Joan Bishop's New Zealand

Crockpot and

Slow Cooker

Cookbook

By the same author:
The New Zealand Food Processor Cookbook
The New Zealand Electric Frypan Cookbook

The author and publisher would like to thank Sunbeam Corporation and House Wares International (Breville) who provided slow cookers to use in the testing of these recipes. The models used were, Sunbeam Crockpot HP003, Sunbeam Slow Cooker HP003 and Breville Avance Meal Maker SLC 70.

First published 1985 by Whitcoulls Publishers
Christchurch, New Zealand
Reprinted, 1986.

Published from 1992
by John McIndoe Ltd, Box 694, Dunedin, New Zealand.

Published from 2005
by McIndoe Publishers, Box 694, Dunedin, New Zealand.

ISBN 0-476-00627-9

Design and graphics by Tim Murphy.
Printed by Rogan McIndoe Print Limited
Dunedin, New Zealand.

Reprinted 1993
Reprinted 1994
Reprinted Twice 1995
Reprinted 1996
Reprinted 1997
Reprinted 1998
Revised   1999
Reprinted 2000
Reprinted 2001
Reprinted 2002
Reprinted 2003
Revised   2004
Reprinted 2005

Contents

Introduction

I wrote the first Crockpot Cookbook more than 25 years ago. Since then our concept of healthy eating has changed, hence the need for new recipes. The slow cooking scene has also changed with a plethora of slow cookers flooding the market.

Slow cookers have become the cult appliance of the 21st century. They are not all identical. Different sizes, wattages and designs mean they have different heating patterns and some cook at a higher temperature than others. This new edition has cooking times for both crockpot and slow cookers.

With obesity levels rising alarmingly, cooking luscious, low-fat meals becomes increasingly important. Enjoyment of food does not depend on excessive amounts of butter and oil. These mouthwatering but virtually fat-free recipes pare away excess calories and limit fat while enhancing flavour and texture.

Since I wrote the previous edition of this book in the late 90's we have become aware of the importance of eating a low G.I. (Glycaemic Index) diet. This is the reason for the much enlarged section on beans and lentils (the group of foods we are encouraged to eat more of because of their low G.I.). No need to soak beans, simply add to the slow cooker along with the other ingredients, cover and cook.

Most recipes do not require the time-consuming task of pre-browning in a frypan. Combine all the ingredients in the slow cooker, switch on and walk away while dinner simmers throughout the day. I regard the majority as "Fast Food" recipes. Although the cooking time is long, the preparation time is short.

There is something special about the cooking and sharing of food; cooking is a rather futile activity unless there is someone to eat what you have cooked. And so I wish to thank my family and friends whose hearty appetites and lively company have graced our table during the testing of these recipes.

Special thanks to my husband Tony Reay for word processing and proof-reading without complaint and willingly eating both the successes and failures as these recipes have evolved. His constant support and encouragement have been invaluable.

Important Information

Pre-heating

Placing food in a warm cooker means that the temperature at which the food starts to cook will be reached more quickly. It is absolutely essential that the slow cooker is pre-heated when baking and when adding hot liquid to the cooker, as the ceramic liner could crack if not heated.

Thickening

The dish can be thickened either at the beginning or at the end of cooking. Use flour at the beginning or stir in a cornflour paste at the end. The liquid used to make the paste need not be water. Chicken, beef or vegetable stock, wines, spirits or juices all add extra flavour. Once the cornflour paste is stirred in, turn the control to high and cook for another 20-40 minutes. Or drain the liquid into a saucepan, add the cornflour paste and bring to the boil on the stove or in a microwave, stirring until smooth and thickened.

How full?

Slow cookers have side coil heating elements so to heat the food efficiently the cooker should be half to three-quarters full. There should however, be a gap of 3-4 cm between the top of the food and the rim of the cooker.

Cooking time can be critical

Use cooking times as guidelines. Cookers vary. The time that food takes to cook depends on the type of food, the temperature of the food when placed in the cooker, the cut size of the food and how full the cooker is. All will affect the cooking time. In some recipes, particularly those cooked on low setting, the slowness of the cooking means that timing is not so important. Food does not overheat or boil and will not burn. Some recipes have a wide variation in cooking time, e.g. cook on low for 7-8 hours. This indicates that the food will be cooked in 7 hours but an extra hour will not overcook it. However with some recipes timing is critical. This is usually when cooking on high. Vegetables are easily overcooked and breads, cakes and desserts need careful timing.

Stirring

Stirring during cooking is unnecessary on low and only very occasionally needed on high. Vegetable or bean stews are the only recipes which may benefit from a stir after 3 or 4 hours cooking on high. Large oval slow cookers need this stir more than the round cookers.

Browning meat

Browning meat is generally not required. See introduction to Beef, Lamb and Pork section, page 70.

Flavours

Flavours can become diluted with long, slow cooking as none of the liquid inside the cooker evaporates off. More seasoning is needed than in other methods of cooking. Dried herbs are best added at the beginning of the cooking whereas fresh herbs give more pizzazz when added during the final 30 minutes.

Add both in greater quantities than you would normally use. Before serving, taste and if necessary add more seasoning.

Dried beans and lentils

The slow cooker is the best way of cooking dried beans and lentils that I know of. No pre-soaking is needed. See introduction to Dried Beans and Lentils section, page 40.

Trivet

A trivet is required in a number of recipes to raise the dish off the bottom of the cooker, allowing a better circulation of air or water. If a trivet is not available use the screw-top ring of a preserving jar, an upturned saucer or a metal biscuit cutter.

Adapting your own recipes

When adapting your own recipes, reduce the amount of liquid in the conventional recipe by half. Little or no evaporation takes place during slow cooking and about a cup of extra liquid accumulates in the cooker during the long slow cook.

Lifting the lid

To avoid heat loss, refrain from lifting the lid during the first three-quarters of the cooking time. Remove the lid only to stir or check for doneness.

Frozen foods

Frozen foods should be thoroughly thawed before being placed in the cooker. As frozen food has been blanched, the cooking time for this is less than for fresh. Usually, thawed frozen vegetables are added towards the end of the cooking period.

Soups

A first-rate soup is more creative than a second-rate painting.
Abraham Maslow (1908-1970)

The slow cooker is an ideal vessel for cooking soups. Almost all soups, because they contain vegetables, dried beans and lentils, need to be cooked on high. Dried beans do not need soaking prior to cooking. They can be added to the cooker with the other ingredients. More detailed information about cooking dried beans and lentils is given on pages 40 and 41.

Once the cooking of a bean soup is complete, if it's not as thick as you would like, mash up or puree some of the liquid and beans in a food processor or blender, then stir back into the soup.

Don't overfill the cooker. There should be a gap of 3-4 cm between the level of the food and the rim of the cooker.

Bean and Vegetable Soup

Crockpot High 8-9 hrs	Slow Cooker High 7 ½ - 8hrs

220g dried haricot beans, washed

1 large parsnip (300g), peeled

2 medium carrots (250g), peeled

1 large onion, finely chopped

2 cloves garlic, crushed

½ cup tomato paste

1 x 400g tin tomatoes, chopped or mashed

¼-½ tsp cayenne pepper

1 tsp brown sugar

2 tsp dried basil

6 cups beef or vegetable stock, hot

salt

grated Parmesan cheese, to serve

Serves 8-9

A hearty, chunky soup which makes a perfect one-dish meal for a cold winter's night. I have made this soup with black beans and black-eyed beans in place of the haricot. The black beans turn the soup a steely grey-black colour which is not unattractive, just different.

1. Pre-heat the cooker for 20 minutes.

2. Place the well-drained beans in the cooker.

3. Chop the parsnip and carrots into small dice (1 cm) and place in the cooker.

4. Add the onion, garlic, tomato paste, tomatoes, cayenne pepper, brown sugar, basil and beef stock. Stir well.

5. Cover with lid and cook following the times and settings above.

6. Check seasoning, adding salt if necessary.

7. Ladle the soup into bowls and sprinkle with grated cheese.

Notes

Potato and Corn Chowder

Crockpot High 6 ½-7 ½ hrs	Slow Cooker High 6 ½-7 ½ hrs

1 onion, finely chopped

3 large potatoes (600g) peeled and cut into 1 cm dice

1 red capsicum, diced

500g frozen corn kernels, (thawed)

2 tsp paprika

6 cups chicken stock, hot

½ tsp finely chopped fresh chilli, or commercially prepared chilli

2 Tbsp butter

¼ cup flour

1 ¼ cups milk

salt

¼ cup chopped fresh herbs to garnish

Serves 8

Delicious and substantial, this homely soup is a meal-in-a-bowl, especially if served with hot crusty bread.

1. Pre-heat the crockpot for 20 minutes.

2. Combine onion, potatoes, capsicum and corn in the cooker and stir well to combine.

3. Sprinkle the paprika over the vegetables and add the chicken stock and chilli and stir.

4. Cover with lid and cook following the times and settings above.

5. Melt the butter in a small saucepan, add flour, cook for 1 minute stirring constantly. Gradually stir in the milk, stirring constantly over heat (or microwave on HIGH for 3 minutes) or until the mixture boils and thickens. Stir into the chowder in the cooker until the mixture is well combined.

6. Check seasoning, adding salt if necessary.

7. Serve hot sprinkled with chopped herbs.

Notes

Beef, Bacon and Shiitake Mushroom Soup

Crockpot High 5-6 hrs	Slow Cooker High 5-6 hrs

250g rump steak

30g dried shiitake mushrooms

1 cup warm water

1 large onion, finely chopped

2 cloves garlic, crushed

3 rashers lean bacon, trimmed and diced

3 medium potatoes (600g) peeled and cubed 1 cm

1 x 400g tin tomatoes, chopped

5 cups beef stock, hot

200g Portabello mushrooms, sliced thinly

Serves 8

The deliciously aromatic liquid of this soup is chock full of flavourful surprises; tender strips of beef, diced bacon, cubed potato, sliced cultivated mushrooms and shiitake mushrooms. Serve with a good crusty bread and this is a complete meal in itself.

Dried shiitake mushrooms are available in oriental stores and many large supermarkets. They need to be soaked in warm water for at least half an hour before using. The stalks are tough and woody. Discard once soaked. Do not throw out the soaking water which is full of flavour. Add it to the soup.

1. Pre-heat the cooker for 20 minutes.

2. Remove any excess fat from the steak and set aside.

3. Soak the shiitake mushrooms in the warm water for at least 30 minutes.

4. Place onion, garlic, bacon, potatoes, tomatoes and beef stock in the cooker.

5. Slice the shiitake mushrooms, discarding stems. Add the sliced shiitake mushrooms and the soaking water to the cooker.

6. Cover with lid and cook following the times and settings above.

7. Grill, barbecue or pan fry the rump steak. I usually cook it medium rare as it does continue to cook a little once added to the soup.

8. Cool the steak and slice into thin strips.

9. Thirty minutes prior to the end of cooking time, add the steak and the Portabello mushrooms to the cooker and continue to cook for the final half hour. Serve hot.

Scotch Broth

Crockpot High 5-7 hrs	Slow Cooker High 5-7 hrs

1kg lamb or mutton neck chops

2 large carrots, peeled and finely chopped

1 large onion, finely chopped

1 turnip, peeled and finely chopped

2 stalks celery, finely sliced

½ cup pearl barley

2 bay leaves

6 cups boiling water

1 tsp dried thyme

salt

chopped parsley to garnish

Serves 6-8

Nourishing and inexpensive, this soup is a good basic version of the traditional Scottish recipe.

1. Pre-heat cooker for 20 minutes.

2. Trim neck chops of fat and cut the meat into small pieces. Place the meat and bones in the cooker.

3. Combine remaining ingredients in the cooker.

4. Cover with lid and cook following the times and settings above.

5. Remove any fat from the surface with a spoon or kitchen paper towels. Remove bones and bay leaves and check seasoning, adding salt if necessary.

6. Serve sprinkled with chopped parsley.

Notes

Curried Pumpkin Soup

Crockpot High 5–7 hrs	Slow Cooker High 5-7 hrs

1.25 kg pumpkin, peeled

1 large potato, peeled

1 x 400g tin tomatoes in juice, mashed or pureed

2 onions, finely chopped

freshly ground black pepper

6 cups chicken stock, hot

1 ½ tsp curry powder

2 tsp brown sugar

½ cup "light" evaporated milk or cream

salt

chopped chives to garnish

Serves 8-10

Pumpkin soup with its rich creamy flavour and glorious golden colour is a universal favourite. The "light" evaporated milk has all the rich creaminess of cream but only a fraction of the calories.

1. Pre-heat the cooker for 20 minutes.

2. Cut pumpkin and potato into small pieces (2-3 cm) and place in the cooker.

3. Add tomatoes, onions, pepper and chicken stock.

4. Cover with lid and cook following the times and settings above.

5. Add the curry powder and brown sugar.

6. Puree in a food processor or blender.

7. Return to the cooker and add "light" evaporated milk. Stir well and check seasoning, adding salt if necessary.

8. Reheat but do not boil. Serve sprinkled with chopped chives.

Notes

Smoky Pumpkin and Apple Soup

Crockpot High 5-7 hrs	Slow Cooker High 5-7 hrs

1 kg pumpkin (weighed after skin and seeds removed) chopped into small pieces, 2-3 cm

1 onion, finely chopped

3 Granny Smith apples (500g) peeled, cored and diced, 2-3 cm

1 Tbsp finely chopped root ginger

¾ tsp finely chopped fresh chilli or commercially prepared chilli

5 cups chicken stock, hot

1 ¼ tsp smoked paprika

salt

chopped parsley to garnish

Serves 8

This velvety soup is infused with a delicate smoky flavour. Do not, however, add too much smoked paprika as the flavour of the pumpkin and the apples should be apparent. Soups which are pureed should have thorough cooking before being processed as hard, part-cooked vegetables will result in a lumpy puree.

If Granny Smith apples are not available, use another eating apple, preferably one that's not too sweet.

1. Pre-heat the cooker for 20 minutes.

2. Place the pumpkin, onion, apple, ginger and chilli in the slow cooker and add the chicken stock.

3. Cover with lid and cook following the times and settings above.

4. Cool slightly and puree in a food processor or blender and return to the cooker.

5. Add the smoked paprika and reheat the soup.

6. Check seasoning, adding salt if necessary.

7. Serve hot, garnished with chopped parsley.

Red Lentil and Carrot Soup with Lemon and Parsley Yoghurt

Crockpot High 5-6 hrs	Slow Cooker High 5-6 hrs

1 medium onion, chopped

3 cloves garlic, crushed

1 ½ tsp ground cumin

2 tsp grated or finely chopped root ginger

2 large carrots (300g), peeled and diced, 2 cm

7 cups vegetable stock, hot

300g split red lentils

2 Tbsp lemon juice

salt

Lemon and Parsley Yoghurt

½ cup Greek style, low-fat yoghurt

2 Tbsp chopped fresh parsley

grated zest of one lemon

Serves 6

The lentils, subtly flavoured with cumin, quickly cook to a puree giving this soup a thick and luscious consistency. Lentils do not need soaking prior to cooking but they should be washed thoroughly.

Warm naan or pita bread is a good accompaniment.

1. Pre-heat the cooker for 20 minutes.

2. Combine the onions, garlic, cumin, root ginger, carrots, stock and lentils in the cooker and mix well.

3. Cover with lid and cook following the times and settings above.

4. Add the lemon juice and check seasoning, adding salt if necessary.

5. Cool a little and puree in a food processor or blender. Reheat.

6. In a small bowl mix the yoghurt, parsley and lemon zest together.

7. Serve the soup piping hot with a dollop of Lemon and Parsley Yoghurt swirled on top.

Notes

Bacon and Lentil Soup

Crockpot High 5-7 hrs	Slow Cooker High 5-7 hrs

3 rashers lean bacon, trimmed and chopped into small pieces

1 large onion, finely chopped

2 cloves garlic, crushed

2 carrots, peeled and finely chopped

1 x 400 g tin tomatoes, mashed or pureed

½ cup red wine

1 cup split red lentils

5 cups boiling water

salt

low-fat sour cream to garnish

Serves 4-6

The lentils add a spicy, earthy flavour and texture to this warm, homely soup.

1. Pre-heat the cooker for 20 minutes.

2. Place the bacon, onion, garlic, carrots, tomatoes, and red wine into the cooker.

3. Wash the lentils thoroughly, drain and add to the cooker. Pour in the boiling water and stir.

4. Cover with lid and cook following the times and settings above.

5. Check seasoning, adding salt if necessary.

6. Ladle soup into bowls and swirl in a little sour cream to garnish.

Notes

Bean and Mushroom Soup

Crockpot High 5-6 hrs	Slow Cooker High 5-6 hrs

20g dried shiitake mushrooms

¾ cup boiling water

1 ½ cups baby lima beans, washed and drained

1 large onion, finely chopped

1 x 400g tin tomatoes, chopped

2 Tbsp soy sauce

6 cups beef stock, hot

220g Portabello mushrooms, wiped and sliced thinly

½ cup thick, plain yoghurt to serve

Serves 5-6

Richly flavoured with mushrooms, this soup is so good, yet so simple to prepare. It is one of my favourites.

1. Pre-heat the cooker for 20 minutes.

2. Place the dried mushrooms in a bowl and pour over the boiling water. Let stand 20-30 minutes.

3. Place the lima beans in the cooker. Add the onion, tomato, soy sauce, beef stock and the dried mushrooms and their soaking liquid.

4. Cover with lid and cook following the times and settings above.

5. Forty-five minutes prior to the completion of the cooking, add the Portabello mushrooms. Replace the lid and cook for the final three-quarters of an hour.

6. Serve hot with a tablespoon of yoghurt swirled into each soup bowl.

Notes

Chicken Stock

Crockpot High 5-6 hrs	Slow Cooker High 5-6 hrs
2 or 3 raw chicken carcasses (remove the livers as they can impart a bitter flavour) 1 onion, finely chopped 1 carrot, peeled and finely chopped 2 celery stalks, finely sliced 2 tsp salt large sprig thyme 2 bay leaves boiling water to cover	*The best stock is one you make yourself and it is a simple matter to make good chicken stock. Supermarkets usually have chicken carcasses or frames for sale at very reasonable prices.* 1. Pre-heat the cooker for 20 minutes. 2. Put all the ingredients in the cooker, cover with lid and cook following the times and settings above. 3. Cool, and strain the stock through a sieve.

Beef Stock

Crockpot High 6-7 hrs	Slow Cooker High 6-7 hrs
1 ½ kg meaty beef bones 2 large carrots, peeled and finely chopped 2 large onions, finely chopped 2 stalks celery, finely sliced 2 bay leaves 1 large sprig thyme 2 large stalks of parsley 2 tsp salt 6 black peppercorns 6 whole cloves boiling water	*Home-made beef stock is simple and inexpensive to make. A good stock is the basis of many dishes and the instant stock cubes or powders do not give anywhere near the same depth of flavour.* 1. Pre-heat the cooker for 20 minutes. 2. Chop the beef bones into small pieces (to extract maximum flavour). Your butcher will do this for you. 3. Place all the ingredients into the cooker with sufficient boiling water to barely cover. 4. Cover with lid and cook following the times and settings above. 5. Strain and allow to cool. Skim off any fat.

Lamb and Lentil Broth

Crockpot High 5-7 hrs	Slow Cooker High 5-7 hrs

2 lamb shanks, sawn in half

1 large onion, finely chopped

2 cloves garlic, crushed

2 medium carrots, peeled and diced, 1 cm

1 medium parsnip, peeled and diced, 1 cm

300g lentils, washed and drained

1 ½ tsp ground cumin

1 ½ tsp ground ginger

6 cups boiling water

salt

chopped parsley to garnish

Serves 6

Lamb shanks, vegetables and lentils simmer together to make a hearty, inexpensive soup. Once the cooking is complete, the tender, flavourful meat is removed from the bone and returned to the broth.

1. Pre-heat cooker for 20 minutes.
2. Trim any fat from the shanks and place shanks in cooker.
3. Add the onion, garlic, carrots, parsnip, lentils, cumin, ginger and the boiling water.
4. Cover with lid and cook following the times and settings above.
5. Remove shanks, cut meat from the bone into small pieces and return to the cooker.
6. Check seasoning, adding salt if necessary.
7. Serve hot sprinkled with chopped parsley.

Notes

Ham and Golden Pea Soup

Crockpot High 5-7 hrs	Slow Cooker High 5-7 hrs

500g yellow split peas, washed and drained

1 large carrot, peeled and finely chopped

2 medium onions, finely chopped

300g ham, finely chopped

7 cups boiling water

1 tsp ground ginger

¼ tsp ground nutmeg

salt

low-fat sour cream to garnish

Serves 8-10

Split peas give this soup a lusciously thick consistency, making it a substantial and comforting meal for a chilly winter's day.

Most supermarkets sell offcuts or scrappy pieces of ham off the bone quite cheaply and these are ideal for this soup.

1. Pre-heat the cooker for 20 minutes.

2. Place all the ingredients in the cooker, cover with lid, and cook following the times and settings above.

3. Check seasoning and add salt if necessary.

4. Either serve the soup as it is or puree in a food processor or blender and reheat.

5. Serve garnished with a dollop of low-fat sour cream.

Notes

Kumara and Carrot Soup

Crockpot High 5-6 hrs	Slow Cooker High 5-6 hrs

700g kumara

500g carrots

1 Tbsp finely grated root ginger

2 cloves garlic, crushed

1 medium onion, finely chopped

6 cups chicken stock, hot

1 x 400ml tin "light" coconut milk

salt

chopped chives to garnish

Serves 6-7

Coconut milk gives a smooth richness to this velvety golden soup. I use "light" coconut milk which has 75% less fat than the regular variety.

1. Pre-heat cooker for 20 minutes.

2. Peel the kumara and carrots. As vegetables are slow to cook in the cooker, cut the kumara and carrots into fairly small pieces (about 2-3 cm) to ensure they cook in the recommended time.

3. Place kumara, carrots, root ginger, garlic, onion and chicken stock in the cooker.

4. Cover with lid and cook following the times and settings above.

5. Remove from the cooker and puree in a blender or food processor in batches.

6. Pour pureed soup back into the cooker and stir in the coconut milk.

7. Cover with lid and continue to cook for 30-40 minutes until hot.

8. Check seasoning, adding salt if necessary.

9. Serve garnished with chopped chives.

Kumara and Pumpkin Soup with Peanuts

Crockpot High 5-6 hrs	Slow Cooker High 5-6 hrs

700g pumpkin

700g kumara

1 onion, finely chopped

6 cups chicken stock, hot

¾ cup smooth peanut butter

salt

chopped, roasted, unsalted peanuts to garnish

Serves 7-8

These vegetables complement each other well and the addition of peanut butter gives the soup a rich, smooth flavour and texture. A real winner.

1. Pre-heat the cooker for 20 minutes.

2. Peel the pumpkin and the kumara. As the vegetables are slow to cook in the cooker, cut the pumpkin and the kumara into fairly small pieces (about 3 cm) and place in the cooker.

3. Add the onion and chicken stock, cover with lid and cook following the times and settings above.

4. Remove from the cooker and puree in a food processor or blender in batches.

5. Pour the pureed soup back into the cooker and stir in the peanut butter. Cover with lid and continue to cook on high for 30-40 minutes until hot.

6. Check seasoning, adding salt if necessary. This is a fairly thick soup. If desired, thin with a little milk, cream or chicken stock.

7. Serve hot garnished with a sprinkling of chopped peanuts.

Notes

Leek and Potato Soup

Crockpot High 5-7 hrs	Slow Cooker High 5-7 hrs

3 large leeks (750g)

400g potatoes, peeled and chopped into small pieces (2cm)

black pepper

½ tsp ground nutmeg

7 cups chicken stock, hot

¾ cup hot milk

½ cup "light" evaporated milk or cream

chives, finely chopped

Serves 8-10

This recipe is based on the classic soup of France – Vichyssoise.

1. Pre-heat cooker for 20 minutes.

2. Trim leeks to remove tough tops and outer leaves. Wash thoroughly and slice thinly, including some of the green part. Place sliced leeks in the cooker.

3. Add the potato, pepper, nutmeg and the hot chicken stock.

4. Cover with lid and cook following the times and settings above.

5. Puree the soup in a blender or food processor. Return to cooker.

6. Add the milk and the "light" evaporated milk. Replace the lid and continue to cook on high until the soup is heated through. Do not boil.

7. Serve sprinkled with chives.

Notes

Vegetables

Eat, drink, and love; the rest's not worth a fillip.
Lord Byron. Sardanapalus (1821)

I like crisp, crunchy, lightly cooked vegetables. Slow cooking cannot achieve this result and so I do not recommend using the slow cooker for cooking green vegetables.

Many root vegetables can be cooked very successfully in the slow cooker but they need to be cooked on high.

Frozen vegetables can be added to the slow cooker during the last 30 minutes of cooking time but they must be thawed before adding, otherwise they lower the temperature too much.

Casserole of Pumpkin and Kumara

Crockpot High 3 ½-3 ¾ hrs	Slow Cooker High 3 ¼-3 ½ hrs

400g peeled pumpkin, diced 2-3 cm

400g peeled kumara, (1 large) diced 2-3 cm

1 large red capsicum, sliced

2 medium courgettes, sliced

1 large red onion, finely chopped

3 cloves garlic, crushed

¼ cup tomato paste

1 x 400g tin Italian tomatoes, chopped

3 Tbsp chopped fresh herbs

Serves 6-7

This medley of colourful vegetables is especially delicious with roasts or grills. The pumpkin and kumara cook more slowly than the other vegetables so cut into small dice. The courgettes and red capsicum can be cut slightly larger.

1. Combine the pumpkin, kumara, red capsicum, courgettes, onion and garlic in the cooker.

2. Spoon the tomato paste and the tomatoes onto the vegetables.

3. Stir thoroughly so that the tomato paste and tomatoes are mixed evenly through the vegetables.

4. Cover with lid and cook following the times and settings above.

5. Sprinkle with chopped fresh herbs and serve.

Notes

Carrots with Marmalade and Mint

Crockpot High 1 ¾-2 hrs	Slow Cooker High 1 ¾hrs

450g carrots, peeled and cut into thin rings

vegetable or chicken stock, hot, to cover

2 Tbsp marmalade

1 Tbsp olive oil

2 Tbsp freshly chopped mint

Serves 4-5

Carrots are a great stand-by winter vegetable but if served just plain boiled they become boring.

Marmalade and mint give these carrots real pizzazz.

Choose small carrots as they are more likely to be sweet and tender.

1. Pre-heat cooker for 20 minutes.

2. Scatter the carrots over the base of the cooker.

3. Pour on the hot stock and ensure the carrots are evenly distributed in the cooker.

4. Cover with lid and cook following the times and settings above.

5. When the carrots are tender, drain off the stock and stir in the marmalade, oil and mint.

Notes

Sweet and Sour Pumpkin

Crockpot High Approx 2 hrs	Slow Cooker High 1 ¾-2 hrs

700g pumpkin

1 tsp olive oil

2 cloves garlic, crushed

1 Tbsp raw sugar

½ tsp salt

2 Tbsp white wine vinegar

¼ cup chopped, roasted, unsalted peanuts (optional)

Serves 4

This is a tasty way with pumpkin.

1. Peel pumpkin, cut into 2-3cm cubes and place in cooker.

2. Add oil, garlic, sugar, salt and wine vinegar to the cooker and toss very thoroughly so that the oil coats all surfaces of the pumpkin.

3. Cover with lid and cook following the times and settings above until pumpkin is tender but not mushy.

4. Remove lid and continue cooking for about 10 minutes to evaporate off any liquid remaining in the cooker.

5. Sprinkle with peanuts if using and serve hot.

Notes

Red Cabbage with Apple and Dill

Crockpot High 1 ¾-2 ¼ hrs	Slow Cooker High 1 ¾-2 hrs

½ medium red cabbage (600g)

2 medium dessert apples (300g)

1 small red onion, finely sliced

2 Tbsp honey

2 Tbsp wine vinegar

1 Tbsp butter

½ tsp salt

freshly ground black pepper

1 ½ tsp dill seeds

Serves 6

Timing is more crucial for this recipe than for most. I find 2 hours is perfect but this will vary depending on how thickly the vegetables are cut.

The cabbage should retain a little crispness and the apple slices should remain whole, not cooked to a pulp.

1. Finely shred the cabbage and place in the cooker.

2. Peel, core and slice the apple and add to the cooker along with the onion.

3. In a small bowl combine the honey, wine vinegar and butter. Melt in a microwave or over hot water.

4. Pour this into the cooker and add the salt, pepper and dill seed and toss to mix well.

5. Cover with lid and cook following the times and settings above.

Notes

Parsnip with Apple and Coriander

Crockpot High 1 ¾-2 hrs	Slow Cooker High 1 ¾ hrs

450g parsnip

1 large (220g) dessert apple

chicken stock, hot, to cover

2 tsp raw sugar

¾ tsp ground coriander

1 Tbsp olive oil

salt

chopped parsley

Serves 4

Rich and sweet and given an intriguing freshness by the apple, this is ideal to serve with a casserole.

Choose young, small parsnips as they have a much sweeter, nuttier taste. If possible use a dessert apple like Granny Smith.

1. Pre-heat cooker for 20 minutes.

2. Wash and peel the parsnips. Slice into thin rounds and place in the cooker.

3. Peel, core, and thickly slice the apple and add to the cooker.

4. Barely cover the parsnip and apple with the hot chicken stock.

5. Cover with lid and cook following the times and settings above.

6. Drain off the chicken stock. Sprinkle the parsnips and apples with the sugar and coriander and toss to mix.

7. Stir in the olive oil and check the seasoning, adding salt if necessary.

8. Sprinkle with parsley and serve.

Notes

Ratatouille

Crockpot High 3 ½-3 ¾ hrs	Slow Cooker High 3 ½ hrs

1 large or 2 small aubergines, about 600g

1 large red onion, finely chopped

4 cloves garlic, crushed

2 medium red capsicums, thinly sliced.

2 Tbsp olive oil

2 Tbsp tomato paste

1 x 400g tin tomatoes, chopped

salt and pepper

2 Tbsp chopped fresh thyme

Serves 4-5

During late summer and early autumn these vegetables are at their peak and when combined make a wonderful vegetable casserole.

1. Wash and trim the aubergine and cut into dice about 2-3 cm.

2. Combine the aubergine, onion, garlic and red capsicum in the cooker.

3. In a small bowl mix together the olive oil, tomato paste and the chopped tomatoes until well blended.

4. Spoon over the vegetables in the cooker and stir well to combine, making sure all the vegetable pieces are well coated.

5. Cover with lid and cook following the times and settings above.

6. Check seasoning – you will probably need to add salt and pepper.

7. Sprinkle with the chopped thyme and serve.

Notes

Scalloped Potatoes

Crockpot High 3 ½-4 hrs	Slow Cooker High Approx 3 ½ hrs

1 kg main crop potatoes, not waxy

salt

pepper

1 ½ Tbsp flour

½ cup hot chicken stock

½ cup grated cheese

chopped fresh herbs to garnish

Serves 4 as a light meal.

Potatoes cooked in this way are very popular and quite substantial. Teamed with a green salad they make an excellent casual lunch or supper dish.

Much of the flavour in this recipe is dependent on the quality of the stock. Home-made chicken stock is ideal but failing this, good commercial stock is now available in small cartons from supermarkets.

1. Pre-heat the cooker for 20 minutes.

2. Oil the cooker base.

3. Slice potatoes thinly and arrange in layers in the cooker, season each layer with salt and pepper and sprinkle with flour.

4. Carefully pour the hot stock over the top.

5. Cover with lid and cook following the times and settings above or until the potatoes are tender.

6. Sprinkle with cheese. Cover with lid and cook for 5-10 minutes more.

7. Sprinkle with fresh herbs and serve.

Notes

Honey and Lemon Kumara

Crockpot High Approx 2 hrs	Slow Cooker High 1 ¾-2 hrs

600g kumara

grated zest of ½ lemon

2 Tbsp lemon juice

2 tsp honey

1 Tbsp butter

½ tsp salt

freshly ground black pepper

Serves 4

The timing for vegetable dishes is not as flexible as for many other dishes. The kumara should not be cooked to a mush but remain in whole pieces lightly coated with the lemony syrup.

For this recipe I like to use Golden Kumara as it is such a gorgeous colour and does not discolour once peeled. It has longer, thinner tubers than the red variety and of course the skin and flesh are golden.

1. Peel the kumara and cut into 1cm dice.

2. Place in the cooker and sprinkle with lemon zest.

3. In a small bowl combine the lemon juice, honey and butter and heat over hot water or in a microwave until melted.

4. Pour this mixture over the kumara, sprinkle with salt and pepper and toss to mix.

5. Cover with lid and cook following the times and settings above.

Notes

Light Meals

Chilli Vegetables with Coconut

Crockpot High 6 – 6 ½ hrs	Slow Cooker High 5 ½ - 6 hrs

1 large red onion, diced finely

3 cloves garlic, crushed

600g peeled and seeded pumpkin, diced 3 cm

2 medium potatoes (300g), peeled and diced 2-3 cm

2 medium carrots (200g) diced finely

1 x 400g tin tomatoes, chopped

½-1 tsp finely chopped chilli or commercially prepared chilli

2 tsp finely chopped fresh ginger

2 tsp ground coriander

1 x 400ml tin "light" coconut milk

3 Tbsp ground almonds

salt to taste

½ cup toasted slivered almonds to garnish

Serves 5-6

This is a pretty dish, golden yellow and very fragrant.

The vegetables and spices cook gently together in the creamy, mild coconut milk which is thickened slightly towards the end of the cooking time by the addition of ground almonds.

Serve with a crusty bread and a salad.

1. Place the onion, garlic, pumpkin, potatoes, carrots and tomatoes in the cooker.
2. Add the chilli, ginger, coriander and coconut milk and mix well.
3. Cover with lid and cook following the times and settings above until the vegetables are tender.
4. About half an hour before serving, stir in the ground almonds.
5. Check seasoning, adding salt if necessary.
6. Cover with lid and continue cooking for the remaining 30 minutes.
7. Sprinkle with the slivered almonds and serve.

Cheese and Corn Spoonbread

Crockpot High 3 ½ hours approx	Slow Cooker High 3 hrs approx

140g fine cornmeal

1 tsp baking soda

⅛ tsp cayenne pepper

2 eggs, size 6

⅔ cup buttermilk

1 Tbsp oil

1 x 410g tin creamed corn

Filling

80g Parmesan cheese, grated

50g sundried tomatoes in oil, drained and chopped

Serves 4-5

Spoonbreads are soft, rich corn breads which are best eaten with a spoon. Made with maize flour, milk, butter and beaten eggs they are baked in a casserole and usually served as a side dish. I serve this as a light main course accompanied by a crisp salad and we eat it using a knife and fork.

1. Pre-heat the cooker for 20 minutes.

2. Oil an 18 cm wide, 6-7-cup capacity casserole dish.

3. Mix the cornmeal, baking soda and cayenne pepper in a medium-sized bowl.

4. Beat the eggs, buttermilk and oil in another bowl, add the creamed corn and mix well.

5. Pour this mixture into the dry ingredients and stir until just combined. Do not overmix.

6. Pour half the batter into the casserole dish, sprinkle with cheese and sundried tomatoes. Cover with remaining batter.

7. Cover the casserole dish tightly with foil and place the dish on a trivet in the cooker.

8. Add sufficient boiling water to come half-way up the dish.

9. Cover with lid and cook following the times and settings above.

10. Serve with a crisp salad and a crusty bread.

Country Style Terrine

Crockpot Low 6-7 hrs	Slow Cooker Low 6-7 hrs
High 3-3 ½ hrs	High 3 –3 ½ hrs

4 rashers streaky bacon, trimmed

3 slices wholemeal toast bread

2 cloves garlic

1 medium onion, quartered

1 egg

250g chicken livers

400g pork mince

300g pork sausage meat

¼ tsp salt

½ tsp freshly grated nutmeg

2 Tbsp chopped fresh herbs

salad leaves or fresh herbs to garnish

Serves 6

In this recipe, very modest ingredients are transformed into an impressive terrine good enough for any occasion. Serve with a mesclun salad and French bread.

1. Pre-heat cooker for 20 minutes.
2. Lightly oil a 6-cup capacity casserole dish which will fit into the cooker.
3. Line the dish with bacon rashers.
4. Process the bread in a food processor until finely crumbed. Tip into a large bowl and set aside.
5. Place the garlic, onion and egg into the food processor and process until finely minced.
6. Trim the chicken livers of any membrane and cut each one into 3 or 4 pieces. Pat dry and add to the onions in the food processor bowl. Pulse briefly to finely chop the chicken livers. They are soft and pulverize very quickly so do not overprocess.
7. Tip this mixture into the bowl with the breadcrumbs. Add the pork mince, sausage meat, salt, nutmeg and herbs. Mix well.
8. Pack the meat mixture into the casserole dish and cover tightly with foil. Place dish on a trivet in the cooker. Add sufficient boiling water to come half-way up the dish. Cover with lid and cook following the times and settings above.
9. Lift casserole dish from the cooker, remove foil and leave to cool for about 30 minutes.
10. Cover with plastic wrap or foil and weight the terrine down with 2 large tins of fruit or similar placed on their sides. Chill well.
11. To serve, unmould onto a platter and allow to come to room temperature. Garnish with salad leaves or fresh herbs. Slice thickly and serve with salad and bread.

Egg and Cheese Bake

Crockpot High 3-4 hrs	Slow Cooker High 3-4 hrs

1 ½ cups milk

4 eggs, beaten

2 cups soft breadcrumbs

1 ½ cups grated Edam or Gruyere cheese

½ tsp salt

pepper

⅛ tsp cayenne pepper

chopped parsley to garnish

Serves 4

Light and tasty, this dish makes an ideal family lunch. Serve with garlic bread and a lettuce and tomato salad.

1. Pre-heat the cooker for 20 minutes. Butter the base and sides of a 6-cup capacity casserole dish.

2. Heat the milk in a saucepan or microwave.

3. Place the eggs, breadcrumbs, cheese, salt, pepper and cayenne pepper in the casserole dish. Mix well.

4. Pour the hot milk over the breadcrumb mixture and stir to combine.

5. Cover tightly with foil. Place casserole dish on a trivet in the cooker.

6. Pour enough boiling water into the cooker to come half-way up the sides of the casserole dish.

7. Cover with lid and cook following the times and settings above.

8. Sprinkle with chopped parsley and serve with garlic bread and salad.

Notes

Golden Corn Pudding

Crockpot High approx 2 hrs	Slow Cooker High approx 2 hrs

1 x 420g tin whole kernel corn, drained

4 eggs, (size 6)

½ tsp salt

1/8 tsp cayenne pepper

¼ tsp ground nutmeg

375 ml "light" evaporated milk

¼ cup grated Parmesan cheese

fresh herbs to garnish

Serves 4

This is a delicate and elegant dish. The corn is topped by a velvety smooth custard with just a hint of cheese.

Serve with ciabatta bread and a tossed bitter leaf salad.

1. Pre-heat the cooker for 20 minutes.

2. Grease a 5-cup capacity casserole dish.

3. Place corn in the casserole dish.

4. Beat the eggs, salt, cayenne pepper, nutmeg and the "light" evaporated milk together.

5. Pour this over the corn in the casserole dish.

6. Sprinkle the Parmesan cheese over the top and stir gently to combine all ingredients.

7. Cover tightly with foil and place the dish on a trivet in the cooker.

8. Pour enough boiling water into the cooker to come half-way up the casserole dish.

9. Cover with lid and cook following the times and settings above.

10. Garnish with fresh herbs and serve.

Notes

Pork, Pinenut and Veal Terrine

Crockpot Low 7-8 hrs	Slow Cooker Low 7-8 hrs
High 3 ½-4 hrs	High 3 ½-4 hrs

4 rashers streaky bacon, trimmed

3 slices wholemeal bread, toast thickness

1 medium onion, quartered

2 cloves garlic

1 egg

2 Tbsp brandy

grated zest of one orange

3 Tbsp orange juice

500g pork mince

500g veal mince

2 Tbsp chopped fresh herbs

½ cup pinenuts

fresh herbs to garnish

Serves 8

The flavours of fresh herbs, oranges and pinenuts are to the fore in this elegant terrine.

Veal mince is not available all year round but beef topside is an excellent substitute.

I like to serve this with French bread, tomatoes lightly drizzled with olive oil and marinated olives.

1. Pre-heat the cooker for 20 minutes.
2. Lightly oil a 6-cup capacity casserole dish which will fit into the cooker.
3. Line the dish with bacon rashers.
4. Process the bread in a food processor until finely crumbed. Tip into a large bowl and set aside.
5. Add the onion, garlic, egg and brandy to the food processor bowl and process until the onion is finely minced.
6. Pour this mixture into the bowl containing the bread crumbs, add the orange zest, juice, pork, veal, herbs and pinenuts and mix well.
7. Pack the meat mixture into the dish.
8. Cover tightly with foil and place the casserole dish on a trivet in the cooker.
9. Add sufficient boiling water to come half-way up the dish.
10. Cover with lid and cook following the times and settings above.
11. Lift dish from the cooker, remove foil, and allow to cool for about an hour.
12. Re-cover with foil and weight it down with 2 large tins of fruit or similar placed on their sides. Chill well.
13. To serve, unmould onto a platter and allow to come to room temperature. Garnish with fresh herbs. Cut into thick slices and serve.

Sunny Brunch Eggs with Brie

Crockpot High 45-55 minutes	Slow Cooker High 40-50 minutes

**Ingredients given for
1 portion**

1 Tbsp finely chopped
sundried tomatoes in oil,
well drained

2 eggs

1 Tbsp chopped chives or
parsley

3-4 very thin slices of Brie

salt and freshly ground
pepper to taste

Serves 1

*This jazzed up version of baked eggs
makes a very special breakfast or
lunch.*

*Six or eight individual ramekins will
fit into a cooker. If they will not all fit
on the base, arrange the dishes so that
two or three are balanced on the ones
below.*

1. Pre-heat the cooker for 20 minutes.
2. For each serving, place the sundried tomatoes in a 7-8 cm ramekin dish.
3. Break the eggs on top, sprinkle with chives and cover with slices of Brie.
4. Sprinkle with salt and pepper.
5. Arrange the ramekins to fit on the base of the cooker.
6. Pour enough boiling water to come half-way up the sides of the bottom layer of ramekins.
7. Cover with lid and cook following the times and settings above.
8. Serve immediately.

Notes

Dried Beans and Lentils

Tell me what you eat, and I'll tell you what you are.

Anthelme Brillat-Savarin

The slow cooker is the best way of cooking dried beans and lentils that I know of. No pre-soaking is required.

Cooking times for dried beans vary with the specific bean, its age and water content. In general, baby lima beans, haricot beans and black eyed beans take less cooking time than black beans, red kidney beans and chick-peas. The addition of salt and acidic ingredients such as tomatoes does not seem to slow down the cooking.

I don't think it is worth cooking less than 450g of beans at a time – this equates to 6 cups of cooked beans. When cool I set aside the amount needed for the dish I am making and freeze the remainder in 2-3 cup lots for future use.

Red Kidney Beans. These may contain a potentially dangerous toxin which is easily destroyed by boiling for ten minutes in a saucepan prior to cooking in the slow cooker.

The cooking times for dried beans are similar whether cooked in the slow cooker or crockpot.

To cook dried beans

1. Pre-heat the cooker for 20 minutes.

2. Place the washed and drained beans in the cooker and add 6 cups of very hot water. Cover with lid and cook on high for the time indicated.

3. Start checking to see if the beans are cooked about 30 minutes before the suggested cooking time has elapsed.

Cook for 2 ¼-4 ¾ hours (depending on type and age of the beans) until tender but still holding their shape. If planning to mash or puree the beans, cook until a little softer. Pour into a colander and drain.

Some approximate cooking times

450g baby lima beans, 2 ¼-2 ½ hrs on high

450g haricot beans, 3 ¼-3 ½ hrs on high

450g black eyed beans, 2 ½-3 hrs on high

450g black beans, 2 ¾-3 ¼ hrs on high

450g chick-peas, 4-4 ¾ hrs on high

450g red kidney beans, 3-3 ¼ hrs on high following an initial 10 minutes boiling in a saucepan.

Spicy Potatoes with Yellow Split Peas

Crockpot High 5 ½- 6 hrs approx	Slow Cooker High 5-5 ½ hrs

1 ½ cups yellow split peas, washed

1 Tbsp olive oil

2 Tbsp black mustard seeds

2 medium onions, sliced

1 tsp ground cumin

2 tsp ground coriander

¾-1 tsp finely chopped fresh chilli or commercially prepared chilli

800g potatoes, peeled and cut into 2 cm dice

3 ¼ cups vegetable stock, hot

¼ cup chopped fresh mint to garnish

Serves 4-6

This ridiculously inexpensive mixture of spiced starches is real comfort food.

The split peas and potatoes are cooked in a fragrant stock, the split peas disintegrating into a delicious mush. The potato chunks absorb the aromatic spices and become tender but do not fall apart. Use a waxy potato such as Nadine so that the pieces of potato stay intact.

I usually serve this with a crisp salad but for a more substantial meal serve with rice or naan bread and offer side dishes as you would for any curry.

1. Pre-heat the cooker for 20 minutes.

2. Drain the split peas and place on the base of the cooker.

3. In a frypan, heat the oil, add the mustard seeds and cover with lid until they finish popping.

4. Add the onions and continue to cook, stirring until golden, about 5 minutes.

5. Add the cumin, coriander and chilli and sauté for a couple of minutes more. Remove from heat.

6. Distribute the potatoes evenly over the split peas.

7. Spread the contents of the frypan evenly over the potatoes.

8. Gently pour the hot stock over the contents of the cooker.

9. Cover with lid and cook following the times and settings above.

10. Sprinkle with the chopped mint and serve.

Ragout of Beans and Mushrooms

Crockpot High 6 ½-7 hrs	Slow Cooker High 6-6 ½ hrs

15g dried shiitake mushrooms

½ cup boiling water

1 large onion, finely chopped

400g potatoes, peeled, cut into 1 cm pieces

1 x 425g tin red kidney beans, washed and drained

½ cup tomato paste

¾ cup red wine

¾ cup vegetable stock

2 Tbsp maple syrup

¼ cup vegetable stock (second measure)

220g Portabello mushrooms, wiped and sliced

low-fat sour cream to serve

¼ cup chopped fresh herbs to garnish

Serves 4-5

This is an irresistible dish, rich with mushrooms and red wine, both of which combine so well with potatoes and sour cream.

Serve with a green salad or a green vegetable.

Use a waxy potato such as Nadine so that the potato does not disintegrate into mush when cooked.

1. Place the dried mushrooms in a small bowl, pour over the boiling water and leave to soak for about 30 minutes or longer.

2. Combine the onion, potatoes, red kidney beans, tomato paste, red wine, ¾ cup vegetable stock, maple syrup and the shiitake mushrooms and their soaking liquid in the cooker and mix well.

3. Cover with lid and cook following the times and settings above.

4. Forty minutes prior to the completion of the cooking add the extra ¼ cup vegetable stock if the ragout looks a little dry. Add the mushrooms and stir gently to combine.

5. Cover with lid and continue cooking for the final 40 minutes.

6. Serve topped with spoonfuls of sour cream and chopped fresh herbs.

Mediterranean Chick-Pea Salad

3 cups cooked chick-peas

50g sundried tomatoes in oil, well drained, finely sliced

½ cup pitted, sliced Kalamata olives

4-6 anchovy fillets, drained and finely chopped

½ cup thinly sliced spring onions

300g cherry tomatoes, halved

fresh coriander leaves to garnish

Dressing

3 Tbsp white wine vinegar

4 Tbsp extra virgin olive oil

1 tsp Dijon mustard

½ tsp salt

½ tsp raw sugar

Serves 4 as an accompaniment.

Dazzling and vibrant flavours abound in this salad. The freshness of the tomatoes and spring onions, the rich oiliness of sundried tomatoes, the saltiness of the anchovies and olives– and the perfect foil for all of these is the nutty, earthy chick-pea.

This salad is ideal as a light lunch for 2-3 people if served with an interesting bread. It is also suitable as an appetizer or as an accompaniment to a main course.

1. To cook chick-peas see page 41.

2. Combine the chick-peas, sundried tomatoes, olives, anchovies, spring onions and cherry tomatoes in a bowl.

3. In a small screw-top jar, shake together the dressing ingredients and pour over the salad.

4. Toss gently and tip onto a serving platter. Garnish with fresh coriander leaves.

Notes

Chilli Bean and Sausage Casserole

Crockpot High 9-11 hrs	Slow Cooker High 8-9 hrs

350g dried pinto beans

250g dried sausage such as chirozo, sliced 2 cm thick

2 cloves garlic, crushed

1 onion, finely chopped

1 x 400g tin tomatoes, chopped

1 tsp finely chopped chilli or commercially prepared chilli

1 Tbsp Worcestershire sauce

1 Tbsp wine vinegar

1 tsp brown sugar

3 ¼ cups beef stock, hot

½ cup red wine

1 red capsicum, cut into strips

1 green capsicum, cut into strips

Serves 6

The spicy flavour of dried smoked sausages blends well with beans and chilli. A lettuce and tomato salad is a good accompaniment.

1. Pre-heat the cooker for 20 minutes.

2. Place all the ingredients except the red and green capsicums in the cooker.

3. Cover and cook following the times and settings above.

4. About 45 minutes prior to serving add the red and green capsicums. Cover with lid and continue cooking for the final three-quarters of an hour.

5. Serve hot.

Notes

Moroccan Chicken

Crockpot Low 8-9 hrs	Slow Cooker Low 7-8 hrs
High 4-4 ½ hrs	**High 3 ½-4 hrs**

6 large chicken legs

2 tsp ground cumin

2 tsp ground coriander

½ tsp allspice

1 large onion, finely chopped

2 cloves garlic, crushed

2 x 300g tins chick-peas or 2 ½ cups cooked chick-peas

2 Tbsp honey

¾ tsp chopped fresh chilli or commercially prepared chilli

¾ cup hot chicken stock

2 Tbsp cornflour

⅓ cup lemon juice

¼ cup raisins

¼ cup chopped fresh coriander to garnish

Serves 6

Plump raisins, lemon juice and Middle Eastern spices enrich this chicken dish. Serve over steamed couscous.

1. Pre-heat cooker for 20 minutes.

2. Remove skin from chicken legs.

3. Combine the cumin, coriander and allspice and sprinkle over the chicken. Set aside.

4. Spread the onion and garlic over the base of the cooker.

5. Rinse the chick-peas and drain well. Place in the cooker on top of the onion and garlic.

6. Arrange the chicken on top.

7. Dissolve the honey and chilli in the hot chicken stock and pour over the chicken.

8. Cover with lid and cook following the times and settings above.

9. Forty minutes prior to the completion of the cooking turn the control to high if cooking on low. Mix the cornflour and lemon juice to a smooth paste and stir into the juices in the cooker. Add the raisins and stir to distribute.

10. Re-cover with lid and continue cooking for the final 40 minutes.

11. Sprinkle with coriander and serve over couscous.

Beans with Oranges and Prunes

Crockpot High 5-6 hrs	Slow Cooker High 4-5 hrs

1 cup dried black-eyed beans

2 medium carrots, peeled and cut into 1cm dice

1 x 400g tin tomatoes, chopped

2 Tbsp tomato paste

½ tsp ground cinnamon

½ tsp ground nutmeg

salt and pepper

grated zest of ½ orange

4 Tbsp fresh orange juice

2 Tbsp fresh chopped marjoram or 2 tsp dried marjoram

2 ½ cups hot vegetable stock

200g button mushrooms, sliced

150g pitted prunes

Serves 4-5

This unlikely combination of ingredients blends to make an unusual and delicious casserole. Serve with a salad and an interesting bread.

1. Pre-heat cooker for 20 minutes.

2. Wash and drain the beans and place in the cooker.

3. Add all the remaining ingredients except mushrooms and prunes.

4. Cover with lid and cook following the times and settings above.

5. Thirty minutes prior to the completion of the cooking add the mushrooms and prunes and stir.

6. Cover with lid and continue cooking for the final half hour.

7. Serve hot.

Notes

Hummus with a Mediterranean Topping

2 cups cooked chick-peas

1-2 Tbsp olive oil

2-3 cloves garlic

5 Tbsp tahini

½ cup lemon juice

1 ½ tsp ground cumin

salt to taste

Topping Ingredients

60g sundried tomatoes in oil, well drained and cut into thin strips

40g pitted Kalamata olives, sliced thinly

60g fetta cheese, crumbled or chopped

¼ cup chopped chives or spring onions

1 Tbsp lemon juice

Chick-peas with their earthy, nutty flavour and firm texture puree superbly to make this seductive Middle Eastern appetizer, hummus. The wow factor with this particular recipe is the topping. Colourful and intensely flavoured, this is sprinkled over the hummus which is spread onto a flat platter to a depth of about 1 ½ cm. The visual impact is stunning, the flavour superb and it adds an extra dimension to an old favourite.

Chick-peas are available dried or tinned (tinned chick-peas have already been cooked). I generally cook 450g of dried chick-peas at a time and freeze them in one-cup lots for later use. Cook chick-peas according to directions on page 41.

1. If using tinned chick-peas, rinse well and pat dry with paper towels.

2. Place chick-peas, I Tbsp oil, garlic, tahini, lemon juice and cumin in a food processor and puree until smooth. Taste and add salt if needed. The mixture should be thick but not stiff. Add the extra oil if necessary.

3. Spoon the hummus onto a flat platter to a depth of about I ½ cm and chill for an hour or so. Bring to room temperature for serving.

4. Combine the topping ingredients together in a bowl and toss well. Scatter this over the hummus and serve with warm pita bread.

Lima Bean Chilli Dip

Crockpot High 2 ¼-2 ½ hrs	Slow Cooker High 2 ¼-2 ½ hrs

To cook the beans

450g baby lima beans, washed and drained

3 large cloves garlic, crushed

1 small onion, chopped

1 tsp freshly chopped chilli, or commercially prepared chilli

1 tsp ground cumin

1 tsp ground coriander

6 cups vegetable stock, hot

To assemble the dip

3 cups cooked baby lima beans

2 Tbsp avocado oil or extra virgin olive oil

2 Tbsp lemon juice

½ tsp freshly chopped chilli, or commercially prepared chilli

½ cup finely chopped spring onion

½ small red capsicum, very finely chopped

60g chopped sundried tomatoes in oil, well drained

salt

fetta cheese to serve

chopped fresh mint to serve

Nicely spiced but not too hot, these pureed beans make a perfect dip to serve with warm pita bread.

It also makes an interesting filling for tacos served with sour cream, grated cheese, and a tomato and shredded lettuce salad.

This dip uses 3 cups of cooked baby lima beans. I don't think it is worth cooking less than 450g of dried beans at a time; this equates to 6 cups of cooked beans. I freeze half of the cooked beans for future use and use the remainder to make the dip.

1. Pre-heat the cooker for 20 minutes.

2. Place the dried beans in the cooker and add the garlic, onion, chilli, cumin, coriander and the hot stock.

3. Cover with lid and cook following the times and settings above.

4. Remove the beans from the cooker and drain well. Divide the beans in half and freeze half for future use. Mash the remaining beans to a chunky consistency.

5. Add the avocado oil, lemon juice and chilli and mix well.

6. Allow to cool and stir in the spring onion, red capsicum and sundried tomatoes. Check seasoning, adding salt if necessary.

7. Spoon onto a rimmed platter or a shallow, wide serving dish.

8. Top with chopped or crumbled fetta cheese and mint. Serve with warm pita bread or crudités.

Spicy Chick-pea and Vegetable Chilli

Crockpot High 4-5 hrs	Slow Cooker High 3 ¾-4 ½ hrs

2 x 300g tins chick-peas or
2 ½ cups cooked chick-peas

1 large onion, finely
chopped

2 large red capsicums cut
into thick strips

3 medium courgettes,
sliced 2cm thick on the
diagonal

400g kumara peeled and
cut 1cm cubes

2 Tbsp chopped fresh basil
or 2 tsp dried

2 tsp ground cumin

½ tsp salt

freshly ground black
pepper

1 x 400g tin tomatoes,
mashed

2 Tbsp tomato paste

1 tsp chopped fresh chilli
or commercially prepared
chilli

2 Tbsp lemon juice

1 cup low-fat sour cream,
to serve

1 ½ cups grated tasty or
Parmesan cheese, to serve

Serves 4-5

Chunky, robust and brimming with a variety of vegetables, this chilli is deliciously filling fare.

1. Wash the chick-peas and drain well. Place in the cooker and add the onion, red capsicum, courgette, kumara, basil, cumin, salt and pepper.

2. In a small bowl combine the tomatoes, tomato paste and chilli and mix well.

3. Pour into the cooker and stir the contents to combine.

4. Cover with lid and cook following the times and settings above.

5. Stir in the lemon juice and adjust seasoning to taste.

6. Serve hot garnished with a dollop of sour cream and a sprinkling of cheese.

7. Serve remaining sour cream and grated cheese in a bowl alongside.

Smoky Bean and Vegetable Hot Pot

Crockpot High 5-6 hrs	Slow Cooker High 4 ¾-5 ¼ hrs

1 ¼ cups dried baby lima beans, washed

1 medium onion, finely chopped

3 cloves garlic, crushed

300g kumara, peeled and diced 3cm

300g pumpkin (weighed after skin and seeds removed) diced 3 cm

1 large red capsicum cut into thick strips

1 large green capsicum cut into thick strips

3 ½ cups vegetable stock, hot

½ cup tomato paste

½ - 1 tsp finely chopped fresh chilli or commercially prepared chilli

1 ½ tsp smoked paprika

¼ cup chopped fresh herbs to garnish

150g low-fat sour cream or Greek style yoghurt to serve

Serves 5

Smoked paprika is an exceptional spice with a truly remarkable flavour. It looks exactly like paprika, bright orangey-red in colour, but it is the smoking of the capsicum as it dries which infuses it with the most extraordinary smoky flavour.

Smoked paprika is available from gourmet food shops and some supermarkets.

1. Pre-heat the cooker for 20 minutes.

2. Drain the beans and place in the cooker.

3. Add all the remaining ingredients except the herbs, sour cream and yoghurt.

4. Cover with the lid and cook following the times and settings above.

5. Sprinkle with chopped herbs and serve topped with spoonfuls of sour cream or yoghurt accompanied by rice or crusty bread and a salad.

Notes

Black Bean and Parmesan Salad

3 cups cooked black beans

1 small red capsicum, finely sliced

½ cup finely sliced spring onions

1 x 410g tin whole kernel corn, drained

¾ cup coarsely grated Parmesan cheese

sprigs of thyme or parsley to garnish

Dressing

3 Tbsp red wine vinegar

3 Tbsp extra virgin olive oil

1 clove garlic, crushed

½ tsp finely chopped fresh chilli or commercially prepared chilli

½ tsp raw sugar

½ tsp salt

2 Tbsp chopped fresh thyme or parsley

Serves 4-5 as an accompaniment.

Black beans, sweet corn and red capsicum contribute to this stunning looking, very flavourful salad.

Perfect served alongside most meat, chicken and fish dishes, it can also be served as a light meal accompanied by a good bread or alternatively as an appetizer.

1. To cook black beans see page 41.

2. Combine the black beans, red capsicum, spring onions, corn and Parmesan cheese in a bowl.

3. In a small screw-top jar shake together the dressing ingredients and pour over the salad.

4. Toss gently and tip onto a serving platter.

5. Garnish with thyme or parsley.

Notes

Bean Tapenade

2 x 400g tins butter beans or 500g cooked lima beans

2 cloves garlic

2 Tbsp drained capers

40g sundried tomatoes in oil, well drained

3 anchovy fillets (20g), well drained

80g pitted Kalamata olives

2 Tbsp olive oil

2 Tbsp lemon juice

2 Tbsp brandy

sprigs of fresh thyme for garnish

Tapenade is an aromatic, very robust puree from Provence, consisting of olives, anchovies and capers.

I've combined these intensely flavoured ingredients with creamy butter beans (lima beans) to lower the GI and calorie count of this very special puree.

Lima beans are available tinned but for some reason are called butter beans. Dried lima beans can be found in health food stores and supermarkets.

If cooking dried lima beans follow directions for cooking dried beans on page 41.

1. Drain and rinse the beans if tinned.

2. Place the beans in a food processor and add the garlic, capers, sundried tomatoes, anchovies, olives, olive oil, lemon juice and brandy and process until smooth, scraping down the sides several times.

3. Transfer the tapenade to a serving dish and garnish with thyme.

4. Serve with pita bread or crudités.

Notes

Cheesy Beans

Crockpot High 2 ½-3 hrs	Slow Cooker High 2 ½-3 hrs

2 x 420g tins Cannellini beans

1 small onion, finely chopped

2 cloves garlic, crushed

1 x 400g tin tomatoes, mashed

¼ cup dry red wine

½ tsp salt

1 ½ tsp dried basil

1 large carrot, peeled and grated

2 tomatoes, skinned and diced

1 green capsicum, finely sliced

½ cup grated Edam cheese

¼ cup grated Parmesan cheese

Serves 4-5

Cannellini beans are white kidney beans, mild flavoured and nutty. During the hour or two in the cooker they take on some of the other flavours in this dish – tomato, red wine, onion and garlic. The beans lose none of their bite or texture during the cooking. Great with a salad.

1. Rinse and drain the beans and place in the cooker.

2. Add the onion, garlic, tomatoes, red wine, salt and basil and mix well.

3. Cover with lid and cook following the times and settings above.

4. Half an hour before cooking is complete, stir in the carrots, tomatoes and capsicum.

   Top with the grated cheeses.

5. Cover with lid and cook for the final 30 minutes.

6. Serve hot.

Notes

Chilli Con Carne

Crockpot Low 9-11 hrs	Slow Cooker Low 8-9 hrs
High 4-5 hrs	High 3 ¾-4 ¼ hrs

1kg chuck or blade steak cut into 2cm cubes

2 onions, finely chopped

2 cloves garlic, crushed

4 Tbsp flour

½ tsp cayenne pepper

2 tsp paprika

1 tsp ground cumin

½ tsp salt

1 x 400g tin tomatoes, chopped

⅓ cup tomato paste

¼ cup red wine

2 x 310g tins red kidney beans

Serves 6

This wonderful savoury mix of chilli, meat and beans, which originated in Texas, works particularly well in the cooker.

1. Combine the meat, onions and garlic in the cooker and sprinkle with the flour, cayenne pepper, paprika, cumin and salt. Toss together.

2. In a small bowl, mix the tomatoes, tomato paste and wine and pour over the meat and onions in the cooker and stir to combine.

3. Cover with lid and cook following the times and settings above.

4. Forty-five minutes before the end of the cooking, turn the control to high if cooking on low and add the rinsed and well-drained beans.

5. Cover with lid and continue cooking for the final three-quarters of an hour until the beans are heated through.

Notes

Puy Lentil and Vegetable Casserole

Crockpot High 6-7 hrs	Slow Cooker High 5-6 hrs

1 large onion, finely chopped

3 cloves garlic, crushed

2 medium carrots (250g), peeled and cut into 1 cm dice

250g Puy lentils, washed and well drained

2 medium red capsicums, cut into thick strips

2 medium kumara, (500g) peeled and cut into 2 cm dice

1x400g tin tomatoes, chopped

2 Tbsp finely chopped root ginger

3 Tbsp sweet chilli sauce

3 Tbsp balsamic vinegar

2 cups vegetable stock

½ tsp ground cinnamon

½ tsp ground nutmeg

1 ½ cups whole kernel corn, tinned, or frozen (thawed if frozen)

salt to taste

shaved Parmesan to serve

Serves 4-6

Grey-green Puy lentils with their slight earthiness and mild spicy flavour combine so well with so many other ingredients. Their mealy texture absorbs and mingles deliciously with strongly flavoured vegetables such as onions, garlic and tomatoes.

Puy lentils are more expensive than other grey-green lentils but both hold their shape when cooked so use whichever is available.

1. Place all the ingredients except the corn and Parmesan in the cooker and stir to combine.

2. Cover with lid and cook following the times and settings above.

3. Forty-five minutes prior to the completion of the cooking, add the corn and stir.

4. Cover with lid and continue cooking for the final three-quarters of an hour.

5. Check seasoning, adding salt if necessary.

6. Scatter the shaved Parmesan over the top and serve piping hot.

Chicken

Chicken cooked in the slow cooker is the best I have ever eaten. A whole chicken can be cooked without pre-browning or the addition of any liquid. It emerges moist and tender.

Chicken pieces may be pre-browned in a frypan to eliminate excess fat but I prefer to remove the skin from the chicken pieces and place the chicken straight into the cooker.

Root vegetables and onions take longer to cook than the chicken. When cooking chicken dishes which contain these vegetables, cut the vegetables into small dice 1.5-2cm and place at the bottom or sides of the cooker with the chicken on top. The vegetables will be submerged in liquid and cook more quickly and evenly.

Chicken with Peaches

Crockpot Low 8-9 hrs	Slow Cooker Low 6 -7 hrs
High 4-4 ½ hrs	High 3-3 ½ hrs

6 large chicken pieces, skin removed

2 Tbsp balsamic vinegar

2 Tbsp soy sauce

½ tsp ground nutmeg

2 cloves garlic, crushed

⅛ tsp cayenne pepper

1 ½ tsp powdered chicken stock

1 x 400g tin sliced peaches in juice

2 Tbsp cornflour

3 Tbsp sherry or chicken stock

toasted slivered almonds to garnish

Serves 6

The combination of chicken with peaches is delicious and gives this dish a light, summery feel.

1. Place the chicken pieces in the cooker.

2. In a small bowl combine the balsamic vinegar, soy sauce, nutmeg, garlic, cayenne pepper, powdered chicken stock and the peach juice. Stir until smooth and well mixed.

3. Spoon this over the chicken in the cooker. Cover with lid and cook following the times and settings above.

4. Forty-five minutes prior to the end of the cooking, turn the control to high if cooking on low and stir in the cornflour mixed to a smooth paste with the sherry.

5. Add the peaches, arranging them evenly around the chicken pieces.

6. Cover with lid and cook for the final 45 minutes.

7. Serve sprinkled with the slivered almonds.

Notes

Chicken with Cranberries and Orange

Crockpot Low 8-9 hrs	Slow Cooker Low 6-7 hrs
High 4-4 ½ hrs	High 3-3 ½ hrs

6-8 large chicken pieces, skin removed

3 cloves garlic, crushed

2 Tbsp soy sauce

zest of one orange

1 cup orange juice

4 Tbsp tomato paste

¾ tsp ground cinnamon

⅓ cup marmalade

½ cup dried cranberries

3 Tbsp cornflour

3 Tbsp brandy, wine or water

1 ½ Tbsp chopped fresh mint

Serves 6-8

This is a rather special chicken dish that combines three of my favourite flavours – garlic, orange and tomato. Serve over couscous accompanied by a salad.

1. Place the chicken pieces in the cooker.

2. In a small bowl mix together the garlic, soy sauce, orange zest, juice, tomato paste, cinnamon and marmalade and spoon over the chicken pieces in the cooker.

3. Cover with lid and cook following the times and settings above.

4. Thirty minutes prior to the end of cooking turn the control to high if cooking on low. Stir in the cranberries.

5. Mix the cornflour to a smooth paste with the brandy and stir into the juices in the cooker.

6. Cover with lid and continue to cook for the final half hour.

7. Serve sprinkled with chopped fresh mint.

Notes

Chicken with Vegetables and Parmesan

Crockpot Low 8-9 hrs	Slow Cooker Low 6-7 hrs
High 3-4 hrs	High 3-3 ½ hrs

6 large chicken pieces

2 large carrots (300g), scrubbed and diced small

1 large onion, finely chopped

2 cloves garlic, crushed

⅓ cup flour

1 ½ tsp dried chicken stock powder

1 Tbsp Dijon mustard

3 Tbsp soy sauce

¼ cup dry white wine

2 tsp dried thyme

300g courgettes sliced thinly, on the diagonal

¾ cup grated Parmesan or tasty cheese

Serves 6

This is very simple and delicious. Serve it with rice and a green vegetable or salad.

1. Remove the skin from the chicken pieces.

2. Combine the carrots, onion and garlic in the cooker and sprinkle the flour and the dried chicken stock over the vegetables. Toss to mix.

3. Place the chicken pieces on top of the vegetables.

4. Mix the Dijon mustard to a paste with the soy sauce, add the wine and stir until smooth.

5. Spoon this mixture over the top of the chicken pieces and sprinkle with the thyme.

6. Cover with lid and cook following the times and settings above.

7. Forty-five minutes before the cooking is complete, remove three or four chicken pieces from the cooker and give the carrots and onions on the bottom of the cooker a gentle stir. Add the courgettes and stir again to distribute.

8. Return the chicken pieces to the cooker, cover with lid and complete the final three-quarters of an hour cooking time.

9. Serve the chicken, vegetables and gravy sprinkled with cheese.

Persian Chicken

Crockpot Low 7-8 hrs	Slow Cooker Low 6-7 hrs
High 3 ½-4 hrs	High 3-3 ½ hrs

1 x 2 kg chicken

Stuffing

70g dried apricots, coarsely chopped

3 Tbsp lemon juice

1 small onion, finely chopped

1 small apple, peeled, cored and diced

40g crystallized ginger, chopped

50g currants

½ tsp ground cinnamon

Sauce

¼ cup apricot jam, (chop finely any large apricot pieces)

2 tsp paprika

½ tsp ground cinnamon

2 Tbsp soy sauce

½ tsp finely chopped fresh chilli or commercially prepared chilli

2 Tbsp brandy, water or wine

2 Tbsp cornflour

Serves 6

This is chicken with a difference. The stuffing is definitely eastern in style, rich with fruit, ginger and cinnamon and the sauce is slightly sweet with a hint of chilli. Both complement the chicken well.

1. Remove skin from the chicken and discard. Rinse chicken and pat dry.
2. Soak the dried apricots in the lemon juice while you chop the onion and apple.
3. Combine all the stuffing ingredients and spoon into the chicken cavity and close with toothpicks. Place chicken in the cooker breast side down.
4. In a small bowl, combine the apricot jam, paprika, cinnamon, soy sauce and chilli and mix well.
5. Using a pastry brush spread this over the chicken.
6. Cover with lid and cook following the times and settings above.
7. Lift the chicken from the cooker and pour the liquid which has accumulated in the cooker into a small saucepan. Return the chicken to the cooker, cover with lid and keep the chicken warm while you make the sauce.
8. Mix the brandy to a smooth paste with the cornflour. Stir this into the liquid in the saucepan.
9. Bring to the boil, stirring constantly, reduce heat and simmer for a couple of minutes until the sauce thickens.
10. Carve the chicken and serve with the sauce.

Chicken and Almond Curry

Crockpot Low 8-9 hrs	Slow Cooker Low 6-7 hrs

6 large chicken legs

1 large onion, finely chopped

2 cloves garlic, crushed

2 Tbsp flour

2 tsp ground coriander

1 tsp paprika

½ tsp ground ginger

¼ tsp cayenne pepper

½ tsp salt

¾ cup "light" coconut milk

2 Tbsp ground almonds

3 Tbsp cornflour

1 Tbsp lemon juice

3 Tbsp "light" coconut milk (second measure)

½ cup slivered almonds, toasted

Serves 6

Spices and coconut milk give this curry a truly eastern flavour. I use the "light" coconut milk which has 75% less fat than the regular variety.

1. Remove the skin from the chicken legs.

2. Place the onion, garlic and flour in the cooker and toss to mix. Spread evenly over the base of the cooker.

3. In a small bowl combine the coriander, paprika, ginger, cayenne pepper and salt and mix well.

4. Coat the chicken pieces with this spicy mixture and place them on top of the onion and garlic in the cooker.

5. Spoon ¾ cup coconut milk over the chicken pieces. Cover with lid and cook following the times and settings above.

6. Thirty minutes before the cooking time is complete, turn the control to high and stir in the ground almonds.

7. Mix the cornflour, lemon juice and 3 Tbsp coconut milk to a smooth paste and stir into the juices in the cooker.

8. Cover with lid and continue cooking for the final 30 minutes.

9. Sprinkle with toasted, slivered almonds and serve.

Chicken in the Pot with Herb Cream Sauce

Crockpot High 4 ½-5 hrs	Slow Cooker High 4 ¼-4 ¾ hrs

1 x 1.8kg chicken, skin removed

1 medium onion, peeled and quartered

parsley stalks

2 large sprigs tarragon or thyme

8 black peppercorns

2 medium carrots (350g), sliced into rings

1 medium parsnip (150g) diced 3cm

4 small potatoes (400g) diced 3cm

4-5 cups chicken stock, hot

⅓ cup "light" evaporated milk

3 Tbsp cornflour

1 Tbsp chopped fresh parsley

1 Tbsp chopped fresh tarragon or thyme

salt and pepper

Serves 5-6

A classic chicken and vegetable dish infused with fresh tarragon. If unavailable, substitute fresh thyme or parsley.

Freeze the leftover chicken stock for later use.

1. Pre-heat the cooker for 20 minutes.

2. Place the onion inside the chicken.

3. Place the parsley stalks, tarragon, black peppercorns and vegetables into the cooker. Try to keep the vegetables to a thin single layer on the bottom of the cooker with more arranged around the sides.

4. Place the chicken, breast side down, on the vegetables.

5. Pour on enough chicken stock to barely cover the vegetables. The chicken will protrude above this and will be sitting near the top of the cooker. The chicken does not need to be covered with stock but will cook in the moist heat of the cooker.

6. Cover with lid and cook following the times and settings above.

7. When the chicken and vegetables are cooked, lift the chicken from the cooker and transfer to a large, heated serving plate. Remove the vegetables using a slotted spoon and arrange them around the chicken. Cover with foil and keep warm while you make the sauce.

Continued next page

8. Measure 500ml of the hot chicken stock from the cooker and pour into a small saucepan.

9. Mix the "light" evaporated milk to a smooth paste with the cornflour and stir into the chicken stock in the saucepan.

10. Bring to the boil, stirring continuously and simmer for a couple of minutes until the sauce thickens. Stir in the chopped parsley and tarragon. Adjust the seasoning to taste.

11. Carve the chicken and serve with vegetables and sauce.

Notes

Chicken with Bacon and Mushrooms

Crockpot Low 8-9 hrs	Slow Cooker Low 6-7 hrs
High 4-4 ½ hrs	High 3-3 ½ hrs

6 large chicken legs

3-4 rashers lean bacon, trimmed and chopped into 1 cm pieces

1 large onion, finely chopped

3 Tbsp flour

1 tsp dry mustard

1 x 400g tin tomatoes, chopped

3 Tbsp tomato paste

1 Tbsp dried marjoram

2 Tbsp cornflour

2 Tbsp chicken stock or water

150g mushrooms, sliced

chopped fresh marjoram to garnish

Serves 6

This is quickly assembled and very good. Mushrooms and tomatoes go well with chicken and the bacon imparts a deliciously smoky flavour.

1. Remove the skin from the chicken legs.

2. Place bacon and onion in the cooker.

3. Combine the flour and mustard and coat the chicken legs with this. Sprinkle the remaining flour and mustard over the onion and bacon in the cooker. Stir and spread evenly over the base of the cooker.

4. Arrange the chicken pieces on top.

5. Combine the tomatoes, tomato paste and marjoram and mix well. Spoon this over the chicken in the cooker.

6. Cover with lid and cook following the times and settings above.

7. Thirty minutes before completion of the cooking, turn the control to high if cooking on low and stir in the cornflour and chicken stock mixed to a smooth paste. Add the mushrooms. Cover with lid and continue cooking for the final half hour.

8. Sprinkle with fresh marjoram and serve.

Chicken with Pineapple

Crockpot Low 8-9 hrs	Slow Cooker Low 6-7 hrs
High 4-4 ½ hrs	High 3-3 ½ hrs

6-8 large chicken pieces, skin removed

1 x 450g tin pineapple pieces in juice

1 Tbsp Dijon mustard

1 tsp paprika

⅛ tsp cayenne pepper

1 pkt dried onion soup

2 Tbsp flour

1 Tbsp wine vinegar

Serves 6-8

For those days when time is precious, simply assemble these ingredients in the cooker, turn it on and forget it.

1. Place the chicken pieces in the cooker.

2. Drain pineapple, reserve juice. Place pineapple pieces in the cooker.

3. Combine the mustard, paprika, cayenne pepper, onion soup and flour and mix well. Gradually add the pineapple juice and vinegar and mix to a smooth paste. Pour over the chicken and pineapple pieces.

4. Cover with lid and cook following the times and settings above.

5. If cooking on low, 30 minutes prior to serving turn the control to high. The contents of the cooker will simmer gently and this will thicken the gravy.

Notes

Hungarian Chicken

Crockpot Low 8 – 9 hrs	Slow Cooker Low 6 – 7 hrs
High 4 – 4 ½ hrs	High 3 – 3 ½ hrs

6-8 large chicken pieces

1 medium onion, finely chopped

2 cloves garlic, crushed

¼ cup flour

1 Tbsp paprika

2 tsp dried chicken stock

1 Tbsp dark soy sauce

1 x 400g tin tomatoes, chopped

2 Tbsp tomato paste

1 green capsicum, sliced finely

low-fat sour cream to serve

Serves 6-8

This is a good way with chicken. The green capsicums add colour and crunch and the sour cream imparts a rich creaminess to the sauce.

1. Remove the skin from the chicken pieces.

2. Place the onion and garlic in the cooker.

3. Combine the flour and the paprika and coat the chicken pieces in this. Sprinkle any of the remaining flour over the onion and garlic in the cooker. Toss to mix and spread evenly over the base of the cooker.

4. Place the chicken pieces on top.

5. In a small bowl combine the chicken stock, soy sauce, tomatoes and tomato paste and mix well.

6. Spoon this mixture evenly over the chicken pieces.

7. Cover with lid and cook following the times and settings above.

8. Thirty minutes before cooking time is complete, turn the control to high if cooking on low.

9. Add the green capsicum and stir to distribute. Cover with lid and continue cooking for the final half hour.

10. Spoon on to plates, top with sour cream and sprinkle with a little extra paprika.

Whole Chicken with Tomato and Orange

Crockpot Low 7-8 hrs	Slow Cooker Low 6-7 hrs
High 3 ½-4 hrs	High 3-3 ½ hrs

1 x 2kg chicken

1 orange

1 Tbsp brown sugar

2 Tbsp chopped fresh ginger

2 cloves garlic, crushed

2 Tbsp balsamic vinegar

¼ cup tomato paste

40g sundried tomatoes in oil, well drained and finely chopped

2 Tbsp brandy, water or wine

2 Tbsp cornflour

Serves 6

When I'm short of time but want something a little special this is the recipe I invariably choose. Simple but delicious.

1. Remove the skin from the chicken and discard.

2. Grate the zest from the orange. Place grated zest in a small bowl and set aside. Cut the orange into quarters and place inside the chicken cavity and close with toothpicks. Place the chicken in the cooker breast side down.

3. Combine the brown sugar, ginger, garlic, balsamic vinegar, tomato paste and the chopped sundried tomatoes with the orange zest. Mix well.

4. Using a pastry brush, spread and dab this mixture over the chicken.

5. Cover with lid and cook following the times and settings above.

6. Lift the chicken from the cooker and pour the liquid which has accumulated into a small saucepan. Return the chicken to the cooker, cover with lid and keep the chicken warm while you make the sauce.

7. Mix the brandy to a smooth paste with the cornflour. Stir into the liquid in the saucepan.

8. Bring to the boil, stirring constantly, reduce heat and simmer for a couple of minutes until the sauce thickens.

9. Carve the chicken and serve with the sauce.

Stuffed Roast Chicken

Crockpot Low 7-9 hrs	Slow Cooker Low 6-7 hrs
High 4 hrs	High 3 ½-4 hrs

1 x 1.8kg chicken

Stuffing

1 ½ cups soft breadcrumbs

grated zest of 1 lemon

1 Tbsp finely chopped onion

¼ tsp dried thyme

½ tsp dried marjoram

1 Tbsp chopped parsley

2 Tbsp melted butter

salt and freshly ground black pepper

paprika, to sprinkle over the chicken

Serves 4-5

Quick to prepare, this whole roast chicken is tender and juicy. If you don't have time to make a stuffing, place an apple in the cavity. Serve with creamy mashed potatoes and a green vegetable.

1. Place all the stuffing ingredients, excluding paprika, in a bowl and lightly mix together. If the mixture is too crumbly, a little water or lemon juice may be added. Avoid making the stuffing too moist.

2. Stuff the chicken cavity lightly with this mixture and secure the openings with toothpicks.

3. Place the chicken in the cooker, breast down.

4. Put the paprika in a small fine sieve and sprinkle it gently and evenly over the chicken.

5. Cover with lid and cook following the times and settings above.

Notes

Beef, Lamb and Pork

A good meal makes a man feel more charitable toward the world than any sermon.
Arthur Pendenys (1865-1946)

Pre-browning of meat in a frypan is not necessary for most recipes. However, as sausages tend to be rather fatty, they benefit from pre-browning and any excess fat can be drained off before the sausages are placed in the slow cooker.

Mince, if being cooked as a meat sauce such as a Bolognese sauce, does need to be pre-browned otherwise the mince clumps together and the resulting sauce is very disappointing, mealy and grey. If the mince is to become meatballs, no pre-browning is required. Do choose very lean mince so that the fat content of the finished dish is low.

Trim all meat of excess fat before placing in the slow cooker.

Root vegetables take longer to cook than meat. Cut vegetables into small dice 1.5-2cm and place at the bottom or sides of the slow cooker with the meat on top. The vegetables will be submerged in liquid and cook more quickly and evenly.

Beef

Sausages in Beer

Crockpot Low 5-6hrs	Slow Cooker Low 4 ½-5 ½hrs
High 3-4 hrs	High 2 ½-3 ½ hrs

oil spray

600g sausages

1 large onion, finely chopped

2 medium carrots (250g total) diced 1 cm

2 cloves garlic, crushed

¼ cup tomato paste

1 can beer, 330 ml

¾ tsp finely chopped fresh chilli or commercially prepared chilli

1 ½ cups green peas, fresh or frozen, thawed if frozen

¼ cup chopped parsley

Serves 4

This is simple, robust fare which appeals to both children and adults. The beer imparts a rich, full flavour to the gravy and the alcohol evaporates off during cooking.

1. Pre-heat the cooker for 20 minutes.

2. Heat a frypan to medium high heat, spray with a little oil and cook the sausages until golden brown. Remove from the pan and slice each sausage into 4 pieces on the diagonal. Place sausage pieces in the cooker.

3. Reduce the frypan heat to medium, add the onion, carrot and garlic and sauté for 5 or 6 minutes until the onion is golden and softened. Add the tomato paste, beer and chilli to the frypan, mix well and bring to the boil.

4. Tip the contents of the frypan into the cooker, stir, cover with lid and cook following the times and settings above.

5. Thirty minutes prior to serving, add the peas, stir to combine, cover with lid and continue cooking for the final 30 minutes. Sprinkle with parsley. Serve hot over creamy mashed potatoes.

Venison Ragout

Crockpot Low 8-10 hrs	Slow Cooker Low 7-8 hrs
High 4-5 hrs	High 3 ½ -4 hrs

1.1 kg venison, cubed

1 large onion, finely chopped

¼ tsp ground nutmeg

¼ cup flour

2 tsp dried thyme

½ cup blackcurrant juice, unsweetened

½ cup port

5 juniper berries, crushed

1 Tbsp chopped fresh rosemary

½ cup "light" evaporated milk

salt

sprigs of rosemary to garnish

Serves 4-5

Prime venison steak cooks in a few minutes on a very hot pan or grill. However, the slow cooker comes into its own for the tougher cuts, cooking them to a succulent tenderness.

Juniper berries give a spicy background flavour, blackcurrant juice and port emphasise the gaminess of the venison and they meld together to form this superbly rich sauce.

1. Place the venison and onion in the cooker.

2. Combine the nutmeg, flour and thyme and sprinkle over the meat. Toss to mix.

3. Pour the blackcurrant juice and the port over the meat. Add the juniper berries and the chopped rosemary. Stir the juice and port thoroughly through the meat.

4. Cover with lid and cook following the times and settings above.

5. Ten minutes before serving, stir in the evaporated milk. Cover with lid and complete the cooking. Check the seasoning, adding salt if necessary.

6. Garnish with rosemary and serve with glazed root vegetables and creamy mashed potatoes.

Corn Bread Tamale Pie

Crockpot High 4-5 hrs	Slow Cooker High 3-3 ¾ hrs

550g lean beef mince

1 small onion, finely chopped

1-1 ½ tsp finely chopped fresh chilli or commercially prepared chilli

½ tsp ground cumin

½ tsp salt

⅔ cup tomato paste

1 x 410g tin whole kernel corn, drained

¼ cup beef stock

100g of fine yellow cornmeal

1 cup milk

1 egg, size 6

¾ cup freshly grated Parmesan cheese, to serve

Serves 4-6

Tamales are a Mexican specialty consisting of a cornmeal cake with a sweet or savoury filling steamed inside a corn husk.

Tamale pie, however, is an American derivative which first appeared in recipe books about the time of the First World War when corn, cornmeal and tomatoes in some form (fresh, pureed or tinned) extended the limited supplies of meat.

Easy and delicious, a favourite with children and adults. A crisp green salad goes well with this.

1. Place the meat and onion in the cooker, add the chilli, cumin, salt, tomato paste, whole kernel corn and the beef stock and stir to combine.

2. In a bowl beat together the cornmeal, milk and egg and stir into the meat mixture in the cooker.

3. Cover and cook following the times and settings above.

4. Serve garnished with Parmesan.

Notes

Beef Stroganoff

Crockpot Low 8-10 hrs	Slow Cooker Low 7-8 hrs
High 4-5 hrs	High 3 ½-4 hrs

1 kg blade steak

¼ cup flour

pepper

1 small onion, finely chopped

3 cloves garlic, crushed

1 x 400g tin tomatoes, chopped

3 Tbsp tomato paste

1 tsp dried beef stock

2 Tbsp dry sherry

200g Portabello mushrooms, sliced

1 cup "light" evaporated milk

3 Tbsp chopped fresh parsley

Creamy mashed potatoes or buttered noodles and a green salad to serve

Serves 4-5

This is very simple but good enough for any occasion. The beef is cooked until tender in a tomato-based sauce with a hint of garlic. The Portabello mushrooms added later give a richness and depth to the sauce.

1. Cut the beef into thin strips, dredge in the flour seasoned with pepper and put in the cooker.

2. Add the onion, garlic, tomatoes, tomato paste, dried beef stock and sherry. Stir well to combine all the ingredients thoroughly.

3. Cover with lid and cook following the times and settings above.

4. Thirty minutes prior to serving, turn the control to high if cooking on low and add the mushrooms. Cover with lid and continue cooking.

5. Ten minutes before serving stir in the evaporated milk. Cover with lid and complete the cooking.

6. Sprinkle with the parsley. Serve with potatoes or noodles and a green salad.

Notes

Beef and Macaroni

Crockpot Low 7-8 hrs	Slow Cooker Low 6-6 ½ hrs
High 3-4 hrs	High 3-3 ½ hrs

1 Tbsp oil

2 cloves garlic, crushed

1 large onion, sliced

700g extra lean mince

3 Tbsp flour

2 Tbsp Worcestershire sauce

1 x 400g tin tomatoes, chopped

½ cup red wine

½ cup beef stock, hot

160g Portabello mushrooms, wiped and sliced

200g macaroni, dried

1 cup low-fat sour cream, to serve

¼ cup chopped fresh herbs to garnish

Serves 4-6

This rich, robust tomato and meat sauce is further enhanced by the addition of mushrooms and sour cream.

Serve with a salad or green vegetables.

1. Pre-heat the cooker for 20 minutes.

2. Heat the oil in the frypan and fry the garlic and onion until soft. Add the meat and stir fry, breaking up the lumps until the red colour disappears.

3. Drain off any fat and place meat and onions in the cooker.

4. Add the flour, Worcestershire sauce, tomatoes, red wine and beef stock to the cooker and mix well.

5. Cover with lid and cook following the times and settings above.

6. Thirty minutes prior to serving, add the mushrooms and stir to combine.

7. Cover with lid, turn the control to high if cooking on low and cook for the final half hour.

8. Just prior to serving, cook the macaroni in a saucepan of boiling salted water following the directions on the packet. Drain.

9. Stir macaroni into the cooker.

10. Serve topped with sour cream and sprinkled with chopped herbs.

Beef Olives

Crockpot Low 8-10 hrs	Slow Cooker Low 7-8 hrs
High 4-5 hrs	High 3 ½-4 hrs

700g topside steak cut into thin slices as for schnitzel (6 pieces)

Stuffing

1 ½ cups soft breadcrumbs

100g mushrooms, finely chopped

2 Tbsp melted butter

½ small onion, finely chopped

2 tsp chopped fresh thyme or ½ tsp dried

2 Tbsp fresh parsley, chopped

pepper

milk, a little to mix

Sauce

1 pkt oxtail soup

3 Tbsp sherry

½ cup water

Serves 5

I like my beef olives with plenty of stuffing. I tuck the edges of each beef olive in and secure them with toothpicks, so that the stuffing doesn't ooze out during cooking. If preferred, use mushroom soup instead of the oxtail.

1. Combine the breadcrumbs, mushrooms, butter, onion, thyme, parsley and pepper. Mix lightly until just combined, adding a little milk if necessary.

2. Divide the mixture evenly between each piece of steak and roll up, securing with toothpicks. Fold or tuck the edges over at each end and secure again with tooth picks.

3. Place the beef olives in the cooker.

4. Mix the oxtail soup and sherry to a smooth paste. Add the water and stir to combine. Spoon over the meat in the cooker.

5. Cover with lid and cook following the times and settings above.

6. Remove toothpicks before serving.

Notes

Spiced Beef Stew

Crockpot Low 8-10 hrs	Slow Cooker Low 7-8 hrs
High 4-5 hrs	High 3 ½-4 hrs

1 kg chuck steak

3 Tbsp flour

2 Tbsp brown sugar

1 tsp curry powder

½ tsp ground ginger

½ tsp mixed spice

½ tsp salt

1 Tbsp Worcestershire sauce

2 Tbsp vinegar

3 Tbsp tomato sauce

2 Tbsp sherry

3 Tbsp water

Serves 4

Quick to assemble and so delicious. If possible, plan ahead and leave the meat to marinate overnight in the spicy sauce. I like to serve this with baked potatoes and a crisp green vegetable such as broccoli or green beans.

1. Cut meat into 2 cm cubes and set aside.

2. Combine flour, brown sugar, curry powder, ginger, mixed spice and salt in the cooker.

3. Add the Worcestershire sauce and vinegar and mix to a smooth paste. Then add tomato sauce, sherry and water and stir. Place meat in the cooker and stir again.

4. Cover with lid and stand in a cool place for at least 2 hours or preferably overnight.

5. Switch cooker on and cook following the times and settings above.

6. Serve with potatoes and a green vegetable.

Notes

Spaghetti Bolognese

Crockpot Low 7-8 hrs	Slow Cooker Low 6-6 ½ hrs
High 3-4 hrs	High 3-3 ½ hrs

1-2 Tbsp oil

1 large onion, finely chopped

2 cloves garlic, crushed

3 rashers lean bacon, trimmed and cut into small pieces

1 kg good quality mince

4 Tbsp flour

1 cup beef stock

1 x 400g tin tomatoes, chopped

½ cup red wine

⅓ cup tomato paste

2 tsp dried marjoram

2 tsp dried thyme

½ tsp grated nutmeg

salt and pepper

50-70g (uncooked weight) spaghetti per person

grated Parmesan cheese

Serves 6-7

Many and varied are the recipes for this famous Italian meat sauce. This slow cooker version is rich and tasty and benefits from a long, slow simmer.

1. Pre-heat cooker for 20 minutes

2. Heat I Tbsp oil in a frypan to medium heat and add onion, garlic and bacon. Sauté until the onions are softened.

3. Spoon into the cooker.

4. Add more oil to the frypan if necessary, increase the heat and stir in the mince. Stir frequently until the mince is no longer pink. Pour off any fat.

5. Reduce the heat to medium and sprinkle the flour over the mince and stir to combine. Add the beef stock, tomatoes, red wine, tomato paste, marjoram, thyme and nutmeg and bring to the boil. Simmer for a minute or two.

6. Spoon into the cooker and stir. Cover with lid and cook following the times and settings above. Add salt and pepper if necessary.

7. Cook spaghetti in plenty of boiling salted water until *al dente*, firm to the bite. Drain.

8. Serve meat sauce over the spaghetti and sprinkle each serving with grated cheese.

Ox Tongue

Crockpot Low 10-12 hrs	Slow Cooker Low 9-10 hrs
High 5-6 hrs	High 4 ¾-5 ½ hrs

1 ox tongue (1-1 ½ kg)
1 medium onion, sliced
2 bay leaves
1 Tbsp cider vinegar
6 whole cloves
boiling water

Serves 6

1. Pre-heat cooker for 20 minutes.

2. Place the washed tongue in the cooker and add the remaining ingredients, with enough boiling water to completely cover the tongue.

3. Cover with lid and cook following the times and settings above. Save the cooking liquid if jellying the tongue.

4. When cooked, cut out the undesirable portions of the root end, including any small bones. Remove the skin by slitting from the root end to the tip on the underside. Loosen the skin at the root and peel towards the tip.

Jellied Tongue

Press cooked tongue tightly into a mould. A round cake tin is excellent.

Add 1 Tbsp gelatin to ½ cup cold cooking liquid. When soft, add 1 ½ cups boiling cooking liquid and stir until completely dissolved. Pour carefully into the mould to cover the tongue.

Chill. Unmould onto a flat serving dish.

Notes

Oriental Beef Pot Roast

Crockpot Low 9-11 hrs	Slow Cooker Low 7½-8 ½ hrs
High 4 ½-5 hrs	High 3 ¾-4 ¼ hrs

1.5kg lean pot roast (chuck, blade, bolar or topside)

2 Tbsp soy sauce

1 Tbsp Worcestershire sauce

2 Tbsp sherry

½ tsp ground ginger

2 Tbsp brown sugar

½ tsp dill seed

2 Tbsp cornflour

2 Tbsp sherry (second measure)

Serves 6-8

Easy and delicious.

1. Place soy sauce, Worcestershire sauce, sherry, ginger, sugar and dill in the cooker and mix well. Add the beef and turn it so that the mixture coats all surfaces of the meat.

2. Cover with lid and cook following the times and settings above.

3. Thirty minutes prior to serving, turn control to high if cooking on low. Combine cornflour and sherry and mix to a smooth paste. Stir into the juices in the cooker.

4. Replace lid and continue cooking for the final half hour.

5. Remove meat from the cooker. Slice and arrange on a platter, spooning some of the gravy over the meat. Serve remaining gravy separately.

Notes

Swiss Steak

Crockpot Low 8-10 hrs	Slow Cooker Low 7-8 hrs
High 4-5 hrs	High 3 ½-4 hrs

1 kg chuck or blade steak cut into small serving size pieces

¼ cup flour

freshly ground black pepper

2 medium onions, sliced finely

2 medium carrots cut into thin rounds

¾ cup tomato puree

½ cup good beef stock

½ cup red wine

Serves 6

This wonderfully rich tomato-flavoured braise was fashionable during the early 1960's and then seems to have disappeared from most cooks' repertoires. Warm, comforting braises and casseroles are enjoying a revival and this one is perfect for the cooker.

1. Combine the steak, flour and black pepper in a plastic bag and shake well until the flour coats the meat evenly. Remove meat and set aside.

2. Add the onions and carrots to the flour remaining in the plastic bag and shake thoroughly. Place the onions and carrots in the cooker and shake over them any flour remaining in the bag.

3. Place the pieces of meat on top of the vegetables.

4. Mix together the tomato puree, beef stock and red wine and pour over the meat and vegetables.

5. Very gently push the meat and vegetables around a little so that the liquid flows around all the ingredients.

6. Cover with lid and cook following the times and settings above.

7. Serve with green vegetables or a salad.

Meatballs in Sundried Tomato Sauce

Crockpot Low 6-7 hrs	Slow Cooker Low 5-6 hrs
High 3-4 hrs	High 2 ¾-3 ¼ hrs

700g extra lean mince

1 cup fresh breadcrumbs

1 egg, beaten

3 Tbsp grated Parmesan cheese

¼ tsp cayenne pepper

2 Tbsp chopped fresh parsley

1 Tbsp dark soy sauce

For the Sauce

¼ cup finely chopped sundried tomatoes in oil, well drained

1 ¼ cups good quality beef stock

¼ cup tomato paste

½ small green capsicum, finely sliced

1 small red capsicum, finely sliced

1 Tbsp cornflour

1 Tbsp water

freshly chopped thyme and thyme sprigs, to garnish

Serves 5-6

Quick and easy to prepare, these aromatic meatballs flavoured with Parmesan cheese and cooked in a rich tomato sauce are a favourite with everyone.

1. In a bowl combine all the ingredients for the meatballs.

2. Using your hands, mix gently until well blended. With wet hands form the mixture into balls about the size of golf balls. (Makes about 22 meatballs.)

3. Place the meatballs on the bottom of the cooker with a second layer on top.

4. Combine the sundried tomatoes, beef stock and tomato paste and pour this over the meatballs in the cooker.

5. Cover with lid and cook following the times and settings above.

6. Thirty minutes prior to the end of the cooking turn the control to high if cooking on low and stir in the sliced capsicums. Mix the cornflour and the water to a smooth paste and stir into the sauce.

7. Cover with lid and cook for the final 30 minutes until the sauce has thickened slightly.

8. Garnish with thyme and serve.

Fruity Beef Topside

Crockpot Low 8-10 hrs	Slow Cooker Low 7-8 hrs
High 4-5 hrs	High 3 ½-4 hrs

1.5kg beef topside roast

1 Tbsp honey

1 Tbsp soy sauce

½ tsp ground cinnamon

100g dried apricots

100g pitted prunes

50g raisins

For the gravy

2 Tbsp cornflour

2 Tbsp brandy or dry sherry

1 Tbsp redcurrant jelly

Serves 6

Topside roasts cooked in the cooker were never as tender as I expected. I now place the topside in an oven bag and then into the cooker and the meat emerges superbly succulent.

This is one of my favourite recipes as it is especially easy but always looks impressive.

1. Mix together the honey, soy sauce and cinnamon. Using a pastry brush paint the mixture over the beef, coating all surfaces.

2. Place the meat in an oven bag, seal, perforate the bag and place in the cooker with perforated side of the bag at top to allow steam to escape.

3. Cover with lid and cook following the times and settings above.

4. Three-quarters of an hour before the completion of the cooking, split open the oven bag and remove it, leaving the meat and juices in the cooker.

5. Turn the control to high if cooking on low and add the apricots, prunes and raisins. Push them down in the liquid which should almost cover the fruit.

6. Cover with lid and continue to cook for the remaining 45 minutes.

7. Pour the juices from the cooker into a small saucepan.

Continued next page

Fruity Beef Topside *cont*

8. Leave the meat and fruit in the cooker to keep warm while you make the gravy.

9. Dissolve the cornflour in the brandy. Stir into juices in the saucepan.

10. Add the redcurrant jelly and stirring constantly bring to the boil, reduce heat and simmer until the jelly dissolves and the gravy thickens.

11. Slice the beef, arrange on a platter, spooning the fruit onto the meat. Ladle some of the gravy over and serve remaining gravy separately.

Notes

Family Beef Stew

Crockpot Low 9-10 hrs	Slow Cooker Low 8-9 hrs
High 4 ½-5 hrs	High 4-5 hrs

1 kg chuck or blade steak

3 large potatoes (700g), peeled and cut into pieces 2-3 cm

200g swede or carrot, peeled and cut into pieces 2-3 cm

1 medium onion, sliced thinly

3 Tbsp flour

2 bay leaves

1 tsp dried thyme

1 ½ Tbsp Dijon mustard

2 Tbsp soy sauce

3 tsp dried beef stock

1 ¼ cups boiling water

1 Tbsp cornflour

2 Tbsp water or wine

250g frozen green peas, thawed

fresh thyme leaves to garnish

Serves 5

A complete meal in a pot.

1. Pre-heat cooker for 20 minutes.

2. Trim any fat from the meat. Cut meat into 2 cm cubes.

3. Arrange potatoes, swede or carrot and onion on the base of the cooker.

4. Toss the meat in the flour and place meat on top of the vegetables. Add the bay leaves and thyme.

5. Combine the mustard, soy sauce and beef stock in a small bowl. Add boiling water and stir. Pour this over the meat in the cooker.

6. Cover with lid and cook following the times and settings above.

7. Thirty minutes before the completion of the cooking turn the control to high if cooking on low. Stir in the cornflour and water mixed to a paste and then add the green peas. Stir.

8. Cover with lid and cook for the remaining half hour.

9. Sprinkle with thyme and serve.

Notes

Corned Beef

Crockpot Low 8-10 hrs	Slow Cooker Low 7-8 hrs
High 4-5 hrs	High 3-4 hrs

Here are several options for ringing the changes when cooking this cut which has been the mainstay for many farming families over the years.

Don't consider corned beef as just another weeknight meal. Jazz up the cooking liquid so that the meat when it emerges, meltingly tender, will have absorbed some of the flavours from the medium in which it was cooked.

Liquid is added to the cooker to barely cover the corned beef. If this liquid is cold it takes a long time to get hot enough for the cooking to begin. Heat the liquid in a kettle or microwave until really hot, then pour it over the corned beef in the pre-heated cooker.

I cook the vegetables to accompany the corned beef separately, not in the cooker with the meat.

Traditional Corned Beef

1.5kg corned beef, brisket, silverside or pickled pork

2 onions, peeled, halved and studded with 10 whole cloves

1 Tbsp black peppercorns

3 Tbsp wine vinegar

3 Tbsp raw sugar

hot water

Serves 6-7

1. Pre-heat the cooker for 20 minutes.

2. Rinse the meat in cold water and pat dry.

3. Place the meat in the cooker with the onions, black peppercorns, vinegar and raw sugar and enough hot water to barely cover the meat.

4. Cover with lid and cook following the times and settings above.

Corned Beef Gingered Up

1.5kg corned beef, brisket, silverside or pickled pork

1 x 1.5 litre bottle dry ginger-ale, heated in saucepan or microwave

1 Tbsp ground ginger

1 Tbsp honey

hot water

Serves 6-7

1. Pre-heat the cooker for 20 minutes.
2. Rinse the meat in cold water and pat dry.
3. Place the meat in the cooker and add the ginger-ale, ground ginger, honey and enough hot water to barely cover the meat.
4. Cover with lid and cook following the times and settings above.

Spiced Corned Beef

1.5kg corned beef, brisket, silverside or pickled pork

½-¾ of a 25g packet whole pickling spices

2 Tbsp golden syrup

2 Tbsp wine vinegar

hot water

Serves 6-7

1. Pre-heat the cooker for 20 minutes.
2. Rinse the meat in cold water and pat dry.
3. Place the meat in the cooker and add the pickling spices, golden syrup and wine vinegar and enough hot water to barely cover the meat.
4. Cover with lid and cook following the times and settings above.

Corned Beef with Ale and Orange

1.5kg corned beef, brisket, silverside or pickled pork

1 x 350ml bottle light ale

3 Tbsp maple syrup

grated zest of one orange

1 cup orange juice

hot water

Serves 6-7

1. Pre-heat the cooker for 20 minutes.
2. Rinse the meat in cold water and pat dry.
3. Place the meat in the cooker with the light ale, maple syrup, orange zest and orange juice and enough hot water to barely cover the meat.
4. Cover with lid and cook following the times and settings above.

Sauces to serve with Corned Beef

Once the meat is cooked by whichever recipe you choose, carve into thin slices and serve with creamy mashed potatoes, lightly sautéed cabbage and either Chilli Remoulade Sauce or Horseradish Sauce, recipes given below.

Chilli Remoulade Sauce

½ cup mayonnaise

½ cup low-fat sour cream

1 Tbsp whole grain mustard

½ tsp finely chopped fresh chilli or commercially prepared chilli

2 Tbsp finely chopped spring onions or chives

1 Tbsp finely chopped parsley

1 Tbsp chopped capers

2 Tbsp lemon juice

This French mayonnaise-based cold sauce is usually served with meat or fish. It is also sometimes flavoured with anchovies. If using, add 2-3 finely chopped anchovies to the mayonnaise along with the other ingredients and stir through.

Combine all the ingredients and mix well. Chill.

Horseradish Sauce

150 ml low-fat sour cream

4 tsp commercially prepared horseradish sauce

½ tsp sugar

2 tsp Dijon mustard

1 Tbsp white wine vinegar

Combine all the ingredients, spoon into a serving dish and chill.

Notes

Braised Oxtail with Raisins and Pinenuts

Crockpot High 5-6 hrs	Slow Cooker High 4 ¾-5 ¼ hrs

3 meaty oxtails, jointed (about 1.8kg once the small tail end pieces have been removed)

½ cup flour

olive oil spray

1 large onion, finely chopped

4 cloves garlic, crushed

1 ½ Tbsp dark brown sugar

1 ½ Tbsp finely chopped root ginger

2 Tbsp soy sauce

2 Tbsp balsamic vinegar

1 tsp dried beef stock

1 cup red wine

⅓ cup raisins

3 Tbsp pinenuts

Serves 4-5

Everywhere beef is farmed, oxtail will be available. The older the animal the larger the tail and the chunkier, meatier joints have the best flavour. The small skinny joints are best in the soup pot.

Oxtail comes rather high in fat but with careful trimming this fat is almost eliminated. I prefer to cook this braise a day ahead, chill overnight and remove any excess fat from the surface. Reheat and serve.

As it cooks, the braise develops wonderfully complex flavours and deepens to a dark mahogany colour.

1. Pre-heat the cooker for 20 minutes.

2. Trim off excess fat and roll the pieces of oxtail in the flour. Heat a large frypan to medium high heat. Spray with oil and add the oxtail a few pieces at a time and brown well. Continue to spray with oil when necessary to prevent the meat sticking to the pan.

3. Transfer the browned joints to the cooker.

4. Reduce the frypan heat to moderate, spray with oil. Sprinkle any remaining flour over the onions and add the onion and garlic to the pan and sauté for about 5 minutes until golden.

Continued next page

5. Add the brown sugar, ginger, soy sauce, balsamic vinegar, beef stock and red wine. Stir well and allow to come to the boil. Pour the contents of the frypan into the cooker. Cover with lid and cook following the times and settings above.

6. Once the cooking is complete, if serving immediately, press folded paper towels over the surface to absorb any fat. Stir in the raisins and pinenuts and serve.

7. If cooking ahead of time, refrigerate overnight and next day scoop off any fat which has come to the surface. Reheat and stir in the raisins and pinenuts just prior to serving.

Notes

Beef in Guinness

Crockpot Low 9-10 hrs	Slow Cooker Low 8-9 hrs
High 4 ½-5 hrs	High 4-4 ½ hrs

1.2kg blade, topside or chuck steak cut into 2.5 cm cubes

2 medium onions, finely chopped

2-3 cloves garlic, crushed

¼ cup flour

2 Tbsp tomato paste

salt and freshly ground black pepper

½ tsp ground nutmeg

1 ½ cups Guinness

3 Tbsp cornflour

3 Tbsp Guinness (second measure)

3 Tbsp redcurrant jelly

Serves 6-7

This is a distinctive and vigorous winter dish. The meat is simmered in the dark full-bodied ale which imparts its rich aroma, colour and flavour to the braise. Near the end of the cooking time, redcurrant jelly is added, giving a wonderful sheen to the sauce.

1. Combine the steak, onions and garlic in the cooker.

2. Sprinkle with flour and toss well.

3. Mix together the tomato paste, salt, pepper and nutmeg. Add the Guinness and stir to combine. Pour this over the meat and onions and mix well.

4. Cover with lid and cook following the times and settings above.

5. Thirty minutes before the end of the cooking time turn the control to high if on low.

6. Stir in the cornflour mixed to a paste with the 3 Tbsp Guinness. Add the redcurrant jelly and stir.

7. Cover with lid and cook for the remaining half hour. Serve with freshly cooked noodles and a salad.

Notes

Braised Beef and Vegetables with Cheese and Chive Dumplings

Crockpot Low 9-10 hrs	Slow Cooker Low 8-9 hrs
High 4 ½-5 hrs	High 4-5 hrs

1.2 kg blade steak, cubed

¼ cup flour

1 medium red onion, finely chopped

3 cloves garlic, crushed

300g kumara, peeled and diced 2 cm

250g cleaned, trimmed and sliced leeks

1 x 400g tin tomatoes, chopped

1 Tbsp Dijon mustard

¾ cup red wine

salt

Serves 6

Richly flavoured with beef and red wine plus the gentle sweetness of kumara and leeks, this is a wonderful aromatic dish.

1. Toss the steak cubes in flour. Set aside.

2. Place the onion, garlic, kumara and leeks in the cooker and stir.

3. Add the meat.

4. Combine the tomatoes, mustard and wine and pour over the meat. Stir a little to ensure the liquid flows around all the ingredients but keep the vegetables submerged.

5. Cover with lid and cook following the times and settings above.

6. Check seasoning, adding salt if necessary.

7. Forty minutes before the completion of the cooking, turn the control to high if cooking on low.

8. Prepare and cook the dumplings following the recipe on page 93.

Continued next page

Notes

Cheese and Chive Dumplings *cont*

Crockpot High Approx 30 minutes	Slow Cooker High Approx 30 minutes

200g self-raising flour

70g grated tasty cheese

100mls milk

1 tsp white vinegar

30g melted butter

1 egg, size 6, beaten

3 Tbsp chopped chives

Serves 6

These light and tender dumplings make a delicious topping for many casseroles and soups.

1. Forty minutes prior to serving, turn control to high if cooking on low.

2. In a medium-sized bowl, stir the cheese into the flour and toss to mix.

3. Combine the milk, vinegar, butter, egg and chives and stir into the flour to make a soft dough.

4. Form into 8 dumplings and place on the top of the bubbling stew or soup.

5. Cover with lid and cook for about 30 minutes until the dumplings are puffed and firm to the touch.

6. Serve immediately. Spoon the stew onto the heated plates, topping each serving with a dumpling or two.

Notes

Beef and Sausage in a Tomato Cream Sauce

Crockpot Low 5-6 hrs	Slow Cooker Low 4-5 hrs

oil spray

2 medium onions, thinly sliced

700g lean beef mince

450g sausage meat

2 large cloves garlic, crushed

2 Tbsp flour

1 cup beef stock, hot

3 Tbsp balsamic vinegar

¾ cup tomato paste

¾ cup "light" evaporated milk

¼ cup chopped fresh herbs to garnish

Serves 6

The simple, homely ingredients in this dish appeal to both young and old.

I have substituted "light" evaporated milk for cream in the sauce. It loses none of its rich creamy taste but is much lower in calories.

I serve this over pasta or noodles accompanied by a salad or a green vegetable.

1. Pre-heat the cooker for 20 minutes.

2. Heat a frypan to medium heat, spray with a little oil, add the onion and fry, stirring frequently until lightly golden, about 4-5 minutes.

3. Increase the heat to medium high, add the beef mince, sausage meat and garlic. Stir to break up the lumps. Continue stirring until the meat is well browned, about 7-8 minutes.

4. Pour off any fat. Sprinkle the flour over the meat and stir.

5. Add the beef stock, balsamic vinegar and tomato paste and continue to cook, stirring for 2-3 minutes.

6. Spoon the mixture into the cooker. Cover with lid and cook following the times and settings above.

7. Thirty minutes prior to the end of the cooking time, add the evaporated milk, cover with lid and complete the cooking.

8. Sprinkle with chopped herbs and serve.

Beef in Burgundy

Crockpot Low 9-10 hrs	Slow Cooker Low 8-9 hrs
High 4 ½-5 hrs	High 4-5 hrs

1.3kg blade steak, cubed

250g lean bacon rashers, trimmed and chopped

1 large red onion, sliced thinly

3 cloves garlic, crushed

¼ cup flour

1 ¾ cups red wine

2 Tbsp tomato paste

2 tsp dried thyme

2 Tbsp redcurrant jelly

1 ½ Tbsp finely chopped fresh rosemary

300g Portabello mushrooms, wiped and sliced

salt

chopped fresh thyme to garnish

Serves 6-7

This classic, deeply flavourful beef stew which French cookery is famous for is so simple to make in a slow cooker.

1. Combine the steak, bacon, onion and garlic in the cooker. Sprinkle the flour over the top and stir.

2. Mix the red wine and tomato paste together and pour over the meat in the cooker. Scatter the thyme over the top and stir.

3. Cover with lid and cook following the times and settings above.

4. Half an hour prior to serving, add the redcurrant jelly, rosemary and the mushrooms and stir gently to combine.

5. Turn the control to high if cooking on low, cover with lid and continue cooking for the final 30 minutes.

6. Check seasoning, adding salt if necessary.

7. Scatter with chopped fresh thyme and serve.

Notes

Beef Curry with Cashew Nuts

Crockpot Low 9-10 hrs	Slow Cooker Low 7-8 hrs

1 kg blade or chuck steak

1 large onion, finely chopped

1 Granny Smith apple, peeled, cored and sliced

1 medium carrot peeled, halved lengthways and cut into thin half circles

4 Tbsp flour

2 tsp ground coriander

2 tsp ground cumin

1 tsp turmeric

¼ tsp cayenne pepper

½ tsp salt

¾ cup "light" coconut milk

½ cup roughly chopped cashew nuts

Serves 4-5

This is a mild curry with a rich, creamy sauce. Serve it with rice and a green vegetable or salad. If preferred, lean lamb may be substituted for the beef.

1. Cut the steak into 2 cm cubes and place in the cooker.

2. Add the onion, apple and carrot and stir.

3. Combine the flour, coriander, cumin, turmeric, cayenne pepper and salt and mix well.

4. Sprinkle this over the meat and vegetables in the cooker and stir.

5. Pour the coconut milk onto the meat and vegetables and stir thoroughly.

6. Cover with lid and cook following times and settings above.

7. Thirty minutes prior to serving, turn the control to high and continue to cook for the final half hour. The higher heat helps the sauce thicken a little more.

8. Sprinkle with cashew nuts and serve.

Notes

Lamb

Tomato-topped Lamb Chops

Crockpot Low 7-8 hrs	Slow Cooker Low 6-7 hrs
High 3 ½-4 hrs	High 3-3 ½ hrs

6 lamb leg or shoulder chops

3 Tbsp brown sugar

¾ tsp ground ginger

½ tsp ground nutmeg

4 Tbsp tomato paste

3 Tbsp wine vinegar

2 Tbsp red wine or vegetable stock

4 medium tomatoes

3 Tbsp cornflour

3 Tbsp water or red wine

chopped fresh mint to garnish

Serves 6

Choose lean lamb, hogget or mutton chops for this recipe and trim off excess fat. The cooking times I have given above are for lamb. If using hogget increase by ½ an hour. If mutton, increase by 1 hour.

1. Trim chops of excess fat and place in cooker.

2. Combine brown sugar, ginger, nutmeg, tomato paste, wine vinegar and wine in a small bowl. Mix well and spoon over the chops.

3. Place the tomatoes in boiling water for about 2 minutes to loosen their skins, then peel and slice thickly.

4. Place sliced tomatoes on top of the chops. This ensures that the meat remains moist during cooking and flavours the gravy, too.

5. Cover with lid and cook following the times and settings above.

6. Thirty minutes before the cooking time is complete turn the control to high if cooking on low. Mix the cornflour to a paste with the water or wine and stir into the juices in the cooker.

7. Cover with lid and cook for the remaining half hour.

8. Serve hot, sprinkled with mint.

Honeyed Lamb with Rosemary

Crockpot Low 8-10 hrs	Slow Cooker Low 7-8 hrs
High 4-5 hrs	High 3 ½-4 hrs

½ leg lamb, approx 1.5 kg

2 Tbsp honey

2 Tbsp French mustard

3 tsp ground ginger

½ tsp ground nutmeg

1 Tbsp soy sauce

1 Tbsp chopped fresh rosemary leaves

For the gravy

2 Tbsp cornflour

2 Tbsp sherry

Serves 5-6

Herbs and spices bound together with honey make a wonderful coating for the mildly flavoured lamb, which emerges juicy and tender.

1. Trim the lamb of any visible fat.

2. Mix together the honey, mustard, ginger, nutmeg, soy sauce and rosemary. Using a pastry brush paint the mixture over the lamb, covering all surfaces.

3. Place lamb in the cooker, cover with lid and cook following the times and settings above.

4. Remove the lamb from the cooker and pour the juices which have accumulated in the cooker into a small saucepan.

5. Return the meat to the cooker to keep warm while you make the gravy.

6. In a small bowl mix the cornflour and sherry to a smooth paste.

7. Bring the juices in the saucepan to the boil. Remove the saucepan from the heat and stir in the cornflour paste.

8. Replace the saucepan on the heat and stirring constantly bring to the boil, reduce heat and simmer for a couple of minutes.

9. Slice the meat and arrange on a platter. Spoon over some of the gravy and serve remaining gravy separately.

Leg of Lamb with Mint and Pecan Stuffing

Crockpot Low 8-10 hrs	Slow Cooker Low 7-8 hrs
High 4-5 hrs	High 3 ½-4 hrs

1 boned leg of lamb or hogget, approx 1.8kg (a 2.2kg leg boned out weighs about 1.8kg)

1 ¼ cups day-old breadcrumbs

3 Tbsp chopped fresh mint

½ small onion, finely chopped

½ cup roughly chopped pecans

salt and freshly ground black pepper

2 Tbsp melted butter

2 Tbsp lemon juice (approx)

1 ½ Tbsp balsamic vinegar

2 Tbsp Dijon mustard

¼ cup chopped fresh rosemary

3 Tbsp cornflour

3 Tbsp red wine

Serves 7-8

A fragrant mixture of rosemary, balsamic vinegar and mustard coats the lamb but does not overpower. The stuffing of fresh mint, lemon juice and pecans complements the lamb well.

Most butchers are happy to bone out a leg of lamb but it is a good idea to give them 24 hours' notice.

If hogget is used in place of lamb increase the cooking time by 1 hour on low and ½ hour on high.

1. Trim any excess fat from the leg.
2. Make the stuffing. In a bowl place the breadcrumbs, mint, onions, pecans, salt, pepper, butter and lemon juice and mix together lightly until just combined, adding a little more lemon juice if necessary.
3. Place the stuffing in the cavity in the leg and fold the meat around it, using string to tie into a neat parcel.
4. Combine the balsamic vinegar, mustard and rosemary. Using a pastry brush, brush this over all surfaces of the lamb.
5. Place the lamb in the cooker, cover with lid and cook following the times and settings above.
6. Remove the meat from the cooker. Pour all the juices in the cooker into a bowl. Return the meat to the cooker, replace the lid and keep warm while you make the gravy.
7. Measure 2 cups of meat juices into a small saucepan. Mix the cornflour to a smooth paste with the red wine and stir into juices in the saucepan.
8. Stirring constantly, bring to the boil. Reduce heat and simmer for 2-3 minutes.
9. Slice the lamb, arrange on a platter and ladle over some of the gravy. Serve remaining gravy separately.

Lamb with Tamarillos

Crockpot Low 8-10 hrs	Slow Cooker Low 7-8 hrs
High 4-5 hrs	High 3 ½-4 hrs

1kg lean lamb, cubed

1 large onion, finely chopped

2 cloves garlic, crushed

1-2 Tbsp fresh root ginger, finely chopped

3 Tbsp flour

1 cup hot chicken stock

2 Tbsp lemon juice

2 Tbsp soy sauce

2 Tbsp honey

4 tamarillos, peeled and sliced

Serves 4

Sliced tamarillos add a special piquancy to this lamb casserole. This recipe is enhanced using either home-made stock or the tetrapack variety available from the supermarkets. To skin tamarillos, plunge them into boiling water for two minutes and then peel.

1. Pre-heat cooker for 20 minutes.

2. Place the cubed lamb, onion, garlic and ginger in the cooker.

3. Sprinkle the flour over the top and stir so that the flour coats all the ingredients well.

4. In a small bowl, combine the chicken stock, lemon juice, soy sauce and honey.

5. Pour this mixture into the cooker and gently stir all ingredients together. Cover with lid and cook following the times and settings above.

6. About half an hour before serving, add the sliced tamarillos to the cooker. Cover with lid and continue cooking.

7. If the gravy looks too thin, turn the control to high and thicken by stirring in 2 Tbsp cornflour mixed to a paste with 2 Tbsp water. Cover with lid and cook for another 30 minutes.

Lamb Shanks with Red Wine and Rosemary

Crockpot Low 9-11 hrs	Slow Cooker Low 8-9 hrs
High 4 ½-5 hrs	High 4-4 ½ hrs

6 lamb shanks, cut in half

2 medium onions, finely sliced

2 cloves garlic, crushed

¼ cup flour

2 ½ tsp ground coriander

¼ cup beef stock

¾ cup red wine

2 Tbsp tomato paste

grated zest and juice of 1 orange

2 Tbsp chopped fresh rosemary

Serves 6

Lamb shanks make excellent eating but they need slow simmering in an aromatic liquid to emerge succulent and tender.

Because of its irregular shape, much wider at one end than the other, a shank is not easy to brown in a frypan. I skip this step when cooking them in the slow cooker.

I prefer to cook the shanks the day before I serve them as this allows for any fat to be skimmed off once the dish is cold.

Alternatively, once the cooking is complete, lift the shanks from the cooker and place a double thickness of paper towel on top of the sauce. This will blot up any fat. Replace shanks and serve.

Lamb shanks are usually sold with the leg bone cut in half. When preparing them for the cooker, continue the cut and slice into two pieces.

1. Trim any excess fat from the shanks.

2. Place the onions and garlic in the cooker.

3. Toss the shanks in flour. Sprinkle any remaining flour over the onions and garlic in the cooker and place shanks on top.

4. Combine the remaining ingredients in a small bowl and stir until thoroughly mixed. Spoon this over the lamb shanks.

5. Cover with lid and cook following the times and settings above.

6. Serve with mashed potatoes and a green vegetable or salad.

Lamb Meatballs with Mint

Crockpot Low 6-7 hrs	Slow Cooker Low 5-6 hrs
High 3-4 hrs	High 2 ½-3 ½ hrs

700g lean lamb or beef mince

1 ¼ cups fresh breadcrumbs

2 Tbsp chopped fresh mint

1 Tbsp lemon juice

1 egg, beaten

1 Tbsp soy sauce

For the sauce

¾ cup good quality beef stock

2 Tbsp brown sugar

2 Tbsp wine vinegar

1 Tbsp soy sauce

¼ cup red wine

2 Tbsp cornflour

2 Tbsp redcurrant jelly

mint sprigs to garnish

Serves 5-6

These little lamb meatballs are subtly flavoured with mint. The minty tang leaches out into the slightly sweet, sour sauce giving an intriguing taste.

1. In a bowl combine all the ingredients for the meatballs.

2. Using your hands mix gently until well blended. With wet hands form the mixture into balls about the size of golf balls (makes approximately 24).

3. Place the meatballs in the bottom of the cooker with a second layer on top.

4. Combine the beef stock, brown sugar, wine vinegar and soy sauce.

5. Pour this over the meatballs in the cooker.

6. Cover with lid and cook following the times and settings above.

7. Forty minutes prior to the end of cooking, turn the control to high if on low. Mix the cornflour to a smooth paste with the red wine and stir into the sauce in the cooker. Add the redcurrant jelly and stir.

8. Cover with lid and cook for the final 40 minutes, until the sauce has thickened slightly.

9. Garnish with sprigs of mint and serve over rice or couscous.

Lamb with Lentils, Orange and Ginger

Crockpot High 3-4 hrs	Slow Cooker High 3-3 ½ hrs

700g lean lamb or beef, cubed

1 ½ cups beef stock

1 onion, finely chopped

2 cloves garlic, crushed

¼ cup finely chopped sundried tomatoes in oil, well drained

grated zest of one orange

½ cup orange juice

3 Tbsp tomato paste

2 Tbsp grated root ginger

2 Tbsp chopped fresh herbs

1 ¼ cups red lentils, washed and well drained

salt

chopped fresh herbs to garnish

Serves 5-6

Although hearty, robust fare, this casserole has lovely fresh orange and ginger flavours.

Lentils are used extensively in Middle Eastern and Indian cooking– unfortunately we tend to ignore them. Easy to use, lentils do not need soaking but should be cooked on high in the cooker.

1. Place all the ingredients in the cooker and stir to combine.

2. Cover with lid and cook following the times and settings above.

3. Check seasoning, adding salt if necessary.

4. Sprinkle with fresh herbs and serve.

Notes

Lamb with Peanut Sauce

Crockpot Low 8-9 ½ hrs	Slow Cooker Low 7-8 hrs
High 4-4 ½ hrs	High 3 ½-4 hrs

1 thick end leg of lamb

2 cloves garlic, crushed

2 Tbsp brown sugar

1 tsp ground coriander

2 Tbsp soy sauce

½ tsp chopped fresh chilli or commercially prepared chilli

grated zest of one lemon

4 Tbsp lemon juice

⅓ cup crunchy peanut butter

1 Tbsp cornflour

1 Tbsp lemon juice

Serves 4-5

A pot roast of lamb in an Indonesian-style sauce is a surprising combination but one that works well. Hogget or mutton may be substituted for the lamb but extend the cooking times, an extra hour for hogget and 1 ½ hours for mutton.

1. Trim the meat of excess fat and place meat in cooker.

2. Combine the garlic, brown sugar, coriander, soy sauce, chilli, lemon zest and juice and mix well.

3. With a pastry brush generously paint all surfaces of the lamb with this mixture. Drizzle any that remains over the top of the lamb.

4. Cover with lid and cook following the times and settings above.

5. Thirty minutes prior to the completion of the cooking, turn the control to high if cooking on low. Stir in the peanut butter. Mix the cornflour and lemon juice to a smooth paste and stir into the juices in the cooker.

6. Cover with lid and cook for the remaining half hour.

7. Remove lamb from the cooker. Slice and arrange on a platter. Spoon over some of the sauce and serve remaining sauce separately.

Persian Lamb Tagine

Crockpot Low 8-10 hrs	Slow Cooker Low 7-8 hrs
High 4-5 hrs	**High 3 ½-4 hrs**

1.25kg boneless lean lamb cut into 2-3 cm cubes

2 medium onions, halved and finely sliced

¼ cup flour

¾ tsp ground ginger

1 tsp ground cinnamon

2 tsp paprika

1 ¼ cups vegetable stock

150g dried apricots

3 Tbsp lemon juice

½ cup pinenuts

salt to taste

Serves 6

Tagines are Middle Eastern stews which combine fruits and spices with meat. Lamb has a special affinity with apricots and the ginger and cinnamon add a slightly spicy sweetness to this rich dish.

1. Combine the lamb and the onion and sprinkle the flour, ginger, cinnamon and paprika over the top. Toss well and place in the cooker.

2. Add the vegetable stock and stir to combine.

3. Cover with lid and cook following the times and settings above.

4. Three-quarters of an hour before the completion of the cooking, turn the control to high if cooking on low. Add the apricots and push them down into the liquid in the cooker.

5. Replace lid and continue cooking.

6. Ten minutes prior to the completion of the cooking, add the lemon juice and the pinenuts. Stir well and check seasoning. Add salt if necessary. Cover with lid and cook for the final ten minutes to heat through.

7. Serve over couscous.

Notes

Simple Lamb Pot Roast

Crockpot Low 8-9 hrs	Slow Cooker Low 7-8 hrs
High 4-4 ½ hrs	High 3 ½-4 hrs

forequarter lamb

pkt onion soup mix

1 Tbsp brown sugar

1 tsp paprika

3 Tbsp chopped, fresh parsley to garnish

Serves 4-6

The preparation is minimal but the long, slow cooking ensures the meat is tender and juicy. Hogget and mutton can be cooked this way too. For hogget increase the cooking times by 1 hour on low and ½ hour on high. If cooking mutton increase the cooking time by 2 hours on low and 1 hour on high.

1. Ask your butcher to joint the forequarter so that it will fit into the cooker. If preferred the forequarter can be boned.

2. Remove all excess fat and place the meat in the cooker.

3. Combine the soup mix, brown sugar and paprika and sprinkle over the top of the meat.

4. Cover with lid and cook following the times and settings above.

5. Pour accumulated juices into a saucepan and skim off any fat. Bring to the boil and boil rapidly until the liquid is reduced and slightly thickened.

6. Serve the gravy over sliced meat sprinkled with the parsley.

Notes

Curried Chops

Crockpot Low 8-10 hrs	Slow Cooker Low 7-8 hrs
High 4-5 hrs	High 3 ½-4 hrs

6 lamb or hogget leg or shoulder chops

1-2 Tbsp mild curry powder

2 Tbsp flour

1 large onion, finely chopped

¾ cup chicken stock, hot

1 large Granny Smith apple, peeled, cored and sliced

2 Tbsp lemon juice

¼ cup sultanas

2 Tbsp cornflour

2 Tbsp sherry, wine or water

Serves 6

Lightly curried chops make an ideal family meal which is quick to assemble.

One kg of cubed lamb or hogget may be substituted for the chops.

1. Pre-heat cooker for 20 minutes.
2. Trim the chops of any excess fat.
3. Combine the curry powder and flour and sprinkle this over the chops. Set aside.
4. Spread the chopped onion evenly over the base of the cooker and arrange the chops on top.
5. Pour the hot chicken stock over the chops.
6. Toss the apple slices in the lemon juice and place them on top of the chops.
7. Sprinkle with sultanas.
8. Cover with lid and cook following the times and settings above.
9. Thirty minutes prior to the completion of the cooking, turn the control to high if cooking on low.
10. Mix the cornflour and sherry, wine or water to a smooth paste and stir into the liquid in the cooker.
11. Cover with lid and cook for the remaining half hour.
12. Serve over rice.

Pork

Pork with Prunes and Cider

Crockpot Low 8-10 hrs	Slow Cooker Low 7-8 hrs
High 4-5 hrs	High 3 ½-4 hrs

1 kg lean pork, diced

1 large onion, finely chopped

2 cloves garlic, crushed

4 Tbsp flour

1 large Granny Smith apple, cored, peeled and sliced

½ tsp salt

½ tsp ground nutmeg

1 ½ tsp ground coriander

grated zest of 1 orange

4 Tbsp orange juice

1 cup cider

2 Tbsp soy sauce

150g pitted prunes

chopped fresh parsley to garnish

Serves 6

These wonderfully complementary ingredients mingle together, making this a particularly delicious casserole.

1. Place pork, onion and garlic in the cooker. Sprinkle with flour and toss so that pork and onions are evenly coated with flour.

2. Add apple, salt, nutmeg, coriander, orange zest, juice, cider and soy sauce. Stir to combine.

3. Cover with lid and cook following the times and settings above.

4. About three-quarters of an hour prior to the completion of the cooking, turn the control to high if cooking on low. Add the prunes, cover with lid and cook for the final 45 minutes.

5. Sprinkle with parsley and serve.

Notes

Pork in Satay Sauce

Crockpot Low 8 - 9 hrs	Slow Cooker Low 7 -8 hrs
High 4-4 ½ hrs	High 3 ½-4 hrs

1 kg lean pork, leg or shoulder, cubed

2 cloves garlic, crushed

1 large onion, finely chopped

1 Tbsp finely chopped root ginger

2 tsp ground cumin

1 tsp ground coriander

¾ tsp finely chopped fresh chilli or commercially prepared chilli

2 Tbsp brown sugar

zest of 1 lime or 1 lemon

3 Tbsp lime or lemon juice

3 Tbsp soy sauce

½ cup chicken or vegetable stock

5 Tbsp peanut butter

2 Tbsp cornflour

2 Tbsp water

½ cup finely chopped spring onions or chives, to garnish

Serves 5

A dish heady with the wonderful spicy flavours of Thailand, Indonesia and Malaya. The pork pieces cook until meltingly tender in this rich aromatic sauce.

1. Place the pork pieces in the cooker.

2. Add the garlic, onion, root ginger, cumin, coriander, chilli, brown sugar, lime zest and juice and stir.

3. Combine the soy sauce, stock and peanut butter in a small bowl and gently heat so that the peanut butter melts and makes a smooth paste with the stock and soy sauce. Pour this into the cooker and stir.

4. Cover with lid and cook following the times and settings above.

5. Thirty minutes prior to serving turn the control to high if cooking on low. Mix the cornflour to a paste with the water and stir into contents of the cooker.

6. Cover with lid and continue to cook for the final half hour.

7. Sprinkle with spring onions or chives and serve over rice.

Notes

Hawaiian Pork

Crockpot Low 8-9 hrs	Slow Cooker Low 7-8 hrs
High 4-4 ½ hrs	High 3 ½-4 hrs

800g lean pork

1 small onion, finely chopped

3 Tbsp brown sugar

1 tsp ground ginger

2 tsp paprika

½ tsp dried chicken stock

½ tsp salt

¼ cup wine vinegar

2 Tbsp soy sauce

1 x 450g tin pineapple pieces in juice, drained and juice reserved

½ cup reserved pineapple juice

2 Tbsp cornflour

3 Tbsp reserved pineapple juice

1 small green capsicum, finely sliced

Serves 4

With its sharp, sweet and sour flavour contrasts, this simple pork and pineapple casserole is a great favourite.

1. Cut pork into 2cm cubes, place in cooker and add onion.

2. In a small bowl combine the sugar, ginger, paprika, dried chicken stock and salt. Add the vinegar, soy sauce and ½ cup pineapple juice and mix well.

3. Pour over the pork in the cooker.

4. Cover with lid and cook following the times and settings above.

5. Forty-five minutes prior to the completion of the cooking, turn the control to high if cooking on low. Add the pineapple pieces and the cornflour mixed to a paste with the 3 Tbsp pineapple juice and stir to mix.

6. Cover with lid and continue cooking. Ten minutes prior to serving stir in the green capsicum.

7. Serve over rice.

Notes

Gingered Pork

Crockpot Low 8-9 hrs	Slow Cooker Low 7-8 hrs
High 4-4 ½ hrs	High 3 ½-4 hrs

1 piece of pork leg, about 1.5kg

3 tsp ground ginger

2 tsp paprika

½ tsp ground nutmeg

1 Tbsp brown sugar

for the gravy

3 Tbsp cornflour

2 Tbsp port wine

grated zest of one orange

3 Tbsp orange juice

salt

Serves 6

When roasted conventionally, pork can be disappointingly dry and tasteless. Cooked this way, the meat emerges succulent, tender and full of flavour.

1. Cut the rind from the pork, removing any fat with it. Cook the rind separately in the oven to make crackling if desired.

2. Mix the ginger, paprika, nutmeg and brown sugar together and rub well into the meat.

3. Place the meat in the cooker, cover with lid and cook following the times and settings above.

4. Remove the pork from the cooker and pour the juices which have accumulated in the cooker into a small saucepan and bring to the boil. Return the meat to the cooker to keep warm while you make the gravy.

5. Mix to a smooth paste the cornflour, port, orange zest and juice.

6. Remove the saucepan from the heat and stir in the cornflour, port and orange mixture. Replace the saucepan over the heat and stirring constantly, bring to the boil. Reduce heat and simmer for a couple of minutes. Check the seasoning, adding salt if necessary.

7. Slice the meat and arrange on a platter. Spoon over some of the gravy and serve remaining gravy separately.

Pickled Pork with Fruit and Cider

Crockpot Low 8-10 hrs	Slow Cooker Low 7-8 hrs

1.8kg piece of pickled pork

½ cup maple syrup

750ml cider

2 Granny Smith apples, peeled, cored and sliced

¾ cup raisins

Serves 6-8

This is one of my special favourites and whenever I serve it the response is overwhelmingly enthusiastic. The pickled pork is gently poached in cider and maple syrup, both of which impart their distinctive flavour and aroma to the meat. The apples and raisins add a sharp piquancy which contrasts well with the richness of the pork. Corned beef is also superb when cooked this way.

1. Pre-heat the cooker for 20 minutes.

2. Trim the meat of any excess fat and place meat in the cooker. Add the maple syrup to the cooker. Pour the cider into a suitable container and heat in a microwave or a saucepan on top of the stove until hot.

3. Pour over the meat in the cooker and turn the meat over in the aromatic liquid.

4. Cover with lid and cook following the times and settings above. If convenient turn the meat half-way through the cooking time.

5. An hour and a half before serving, add the apples and raisins. Cover with lid and continue cooking for the final 90 minutes.

6. Remove the meat from the cooker. Slice and arrange on a platter, spooning the fruit onto the meat. Serve, offering Horseradish Sauce or Chilli Remoulade Sauce (recipes on page 88).

Pork Cassoulet

Crockpot Low 9-11 hrs	Slow Cooker Low 8-9 hrs
High 4-5 hrs	High 3 ½-4 ½ hrs

700g lean pork, cubed

2 Tbsp flour

4 rashers lean bacon, trimmed and chopped

2 medium carrots, peeled and diced

3 cloves garlic, crushed

1 x 400g tin tomatoes, chopped

2 Tbsp tomato paste

¾ cup chicken stock, hot

2 bay leaves

1 Tbsp chopped fresh thyme or 1 tsp dried thyme

1 tsp ground allspice

3 x 300g tins butter beans or 3 ½ cups cooked white beans

350g thin pork sausages

chopped parsley to garnish

Serves 6-7

There are many versions of this legendary French dish, all based on dried white beans cooked with a combination of meats. This simple adaptation is tasty, gutsy and perfect for a fireside supper.

1. Pre-heat the cooker for 20 minutes.

2. Place the pork in the cooker and sprinkle with flour. Toss to combine.

3. Add the bacon, carrots, garlic, tomatoes, tomato paste, chicken stock, bay leaves, thyme, allspice and beans and stir.

4. Cover with lid and cook following the times and settings above.

5. About 45 minutes prior to serving, grill or pan-fry the sausages and cut on the diagonal into slices 2-3cm thick. Add to the cooker and stir gently.

6. Replace lid and continue cooking for the remaining time.

7. Check seasoning, adding salt if necessary. Serve sprinkled with chopped parsley.

Notes

Pork Chops with Apple

Crockpot Low 8-9 hrs	Slow Cooker Low 7-8 hrs
High 4-4 ½ hrs	High 3 ½-4 hrs

6 lean pork chops

1 large onion, finely chopped

1 medium kumara (300g) peeled and cubed, 1-2 cm

¼ cup flour

2 Tbsp balsamic vinegar

2 Tbsp soy sauce

1 ½ Tbsp finely chopped root ginger

2 medium (360g total) dessert apples, peeled, cored and sliced

2 Tbsp lemon juice

2 Tbsp maple syrup

1 ½ Tbsp finely chopped fresh rosemary

Serves 6

The sweet, sharp flavours of kumara and apple balance superbly the richness of pork. I prefer to use Golden Kumara in this dish as it does not darken once peeled and the vibrant apricot colour adds great eye appeal.

1. Trim chops of any excess fat.

2. Place onion and kumara in the cooker.

3. Sprinkle the flour over the chops.

4. Sprinkle any remaining flour over the vegetables in the cooker. Stir and spread the vegetables evenly over the base of the cooker.

5. Arrange the chops on top.

6. Combine the balsamic vinegar, soy sauce and root ginger and spoon this over the chops.

7. Toss the apple slices in lemon juice and place on top of the meat.

8. Drizzle the maple syrup over the apples and sprinkle with rosemary.

9. Cover with lid and cook following the times and settings above.

Notes

Desserts

I have chosen only desserts which I think the cooker cooks superbly well and they fall into the following three categories.

Steamed Puddings

The cooker is the ideal way to cook steamed puddings effortlessly and to perfection. The water in the pot does not need to be topped up as it will not boil dry and it is almost impossible to overcook the pudding.

Fruit

Both fresh and dried fruits are very suited to the cooker's gentle heat. Fresh fruits remain intact without boiling to a pulp and the dried fruits plump up beautifully as they absorb the flavours from the liquid in which they are cooking. The long, slow cooking at low temperatures allows the flavours of the various fruits, spices, liquors and other seasonings to blend and mingle so that the resulting compote is a rich amalgamation of all these tastes, with the pieces of fruit retaining their shape.

Baked Custards

The moderate, moist heat of the cooker completely envelops the container in which the custard is being cooked, allowing the custard to thicken to a velvety smoothness. Intense heat will cause the custard to separate and weep.

All Seasons Christmas Pudding

Crockpot High 6-7 hrs	Slow Cooker High 6- 7 hrs

160g dried apricots (preferably Central Otago), chopped

130g dried figs, chopped.

130g crystallized ginger, chopped

130g raisins

100g sultanas

100g soft breadcrumbs

150g plain flour

½ cup brown sugar, firmly packed

1 tsp each mixed spice and ground cinnamon

80g butter or reduced-fat margarine

¼ cup golden syrup

1 tsp baking soda

grated zest of 1 ½ oranges

¼ cup orange juice

2 Tbsp brandy

2 eggs beaten

1 Granny Smith apple, (180g) cored, peeled and grated

Serves 6-8

This is a scrumptious steamed pudding and one of the reasons for its superb flavours is the mix of dried fruits. I love the sharp, strong taste of dried apricots, the voluptuousness of figs and the zing of ginger – all give an intensity of flavour not found in some of the more bland dried fruits. However, other dried fruits may be substituted as long as the total weight is 650g.

Don't wait until Christmas to try this. Serve it throughout the year.

1. Pre-heat the cooker for 20 minutes.

2. Choose an 8-cup capacity pudding basin which will fit into the cooker.

3. Line the base of the pudding basin with non-stick baking paper and grease the sides.

4. In a large bowl, mix together the dried fruit, breadcrumbs, flour, brown sugar, mixed spice and ground cinnamon. Stir well and set aside.

5. Melt the butter or margarine and golden syrup. Stir in the baking soda, orange zest, juice, brandy, eggs and the grated apple. Combine these two mixtures and mix thoroughly.

Continued next page

6. Pack the mixture into the prepared basin, cover with a piece of non-stick baking paper cut to the same size as the top of the basin, and a double sheet of foil. Tie or tuck securely under the rim.

7. Stand the basin on a trivet in the cooker and pour enough boiling water into the cooker to come half-way up the side of the basin.

8. Cook following the times and settings above.

9. Reheat if necessary, allowing 2-3 hours on high.

Turn out onto a serving dish and decorate with holly leaves. If berries are not available, I thread red jubes and jelly beans on toothpicks and nestle them amongst the leaves. Serve with cream, thickened yoghurt, custard or ice cream.

Notes

Butterscotch Pudding

Crockpot High 2 ½-3 hrs	Slow Cooker High 2 ½-3 hrs

220g self-raising flour

¼ cup sugar

2 Tbsp melted butter or margarine

¾ cup milk

Sauce

4 Tbsp golden syrup

1 Tbsp butter or margarine

1 cup boiling water

Serves 4

More like a baked pudding than a steamed one. With its really rich butterscotch sauce this is a perfect family pudding and it is so easy to make.

1. Pre-heat cooker for 20 minutes.

2. Lightly grease a 6-cup capacity casserole dish or pudding basin.

3. Sift flour and sugar into a mixing bowl.

4. Combine melted butter and milk and add to the dry ingredients. Stir until the mixture is well blended. Spoon into the casserole dish.

5. Mix together the ingredients for the sauce and stir until the butter is melted. Pour gently over the pudding mixture.

6. Place casserole dish on a trivet in the cooker. Do not cover the dish or put water around it.

7. Cover the cooker with lid and cook following the times and settings above.

Notes

Steamed Jam Pudding

Crockpot High 2 ½-3 hrs	Slow Cooker High 2 ½ - 3 hrs

4 Tbsp jam

4 Tbsp butter, softened but not melted

¼ cup sugar

1 egg

1 ½ cups plain flour

2 tsp baking powder

½ cup milk (approx)

Serves 6

Easy and economical, this pudding is filling and warming. Ideal for the family on a cold winter's night.

1. Pre-heat cooker for 20 minutes.

2. Lightly grease a 5-cup capacity pudding basin.

3. Spoon the jam into the bottom of the basin.

4. Cream the butter, sugar and egg until pale and fluffy.

5. Fold in the flour and baking powder. Add milk and mix well. The batter should drop from a spoon. Add a little more milk if necessary to get the right consistency.

6. Turn the mixture into the basin on top of the jam.

7. Cover tightly with foil. Place basin on trivet in the cooker.

8. Pour enough boiling water into the cooker to come half-way up the sides of the pudding basin. Cover with lid and cook following the times and settings above.

9. Turn out the pudding and serve with custard, cream or ice cream.

Notes

Granny's Steamed Pudding

Crockpot High 3-4 hrs	Slow Cooker High 3-4 hrs

150g soft breadcrumbs

130g plain flour

110g brown sugar

2 tsp ground cinnamon

220g mixed dried fruit

50g butter

2 Tbsp golden syrup

2 tsp baking soda

1 cup milk

Serves 6-8

Sometimes a very rich Christmas pudding is not wanted. This pudding is light, relatively inexpensive and makes an ideal steamed pudding for any time of the year. My husband Tony enjoys it cut into slices and eaten as cake.

1. Pre-heat the cooker for 20 minutes.

2. Grease an 8-cup capacity pudding basin.

3. In a medium-sized bowl mix together the breadcrumbs, flour, sugar, cinnamon and fruit.

4. Melt the butter and the golden syrup.

5. Add the baking soda and milk and stir.

6. Pour this mixture into the dry ingredients and mix well. Turn into prepared basin. Cover tightly with foil. Place basin on a trivet in the cooker.

7. Pour enough boiling water into the cooker to come half-way up the basin, cover with lid and cook following the times and settings above.

8. Serve with thickened yoghurt, cream or ice cream.

Crème Brulee

Crockpot Low 4-4 ½ hrs	Slow Cooker Low 4-4 ½ hrs
High approximately 2 hrs	High approximately 2 hrs

3 eggs (size 6)

3 Tbsp caster sugar

1 tsp vanilla essence

375ml tin "light" evaporated milk

200 ml standard milk

100g caster sugar (second measure)

Serves 4

This most famous of all custards topped with a layer of caramelized sugar may have originated in France as early as the 17th century. However, the English also have very early recipes for a similar custard called Burnt Cream. It is delicious no matter what the name. I have substituted "light" evaporated milk for the cream as it is much lower in fat but this does not in any way detract from the custard's creamy flavour. Serve with fresh or lightly cooked fruit. The Rhubarb and Strawberry sauce (recipe Page 123) would be perfect.

1. Pre-heat the cooker for 20 minutes.

2. Beat the eggs with 3 Tbsp caster sugar and the vanilla essence until thick and creamy.

3. Add the evaporated milk and the standard milk and beat until thoroughly blended.

4. Strain into 4 ramekin dishes 7-8cm wide.

5. Place the ramekin dishes into the cooker and pour sufficient boiling water into the cooker to come half-way up the sides of the dishes.

6. Cover with lid and cook following the times and settings above.

7. Remove from the cooker and chill.

8. Heat the grill. Sprinkle each custard with 1 ½ Tbsp sugar to form a thin layer.

9. Grill as close as possible to the heat until the sugar melts and caramelizes, 2-3 minutes. Do not overcook as the custard will bubble through the sugar.

10. Chill again but for no longer than 2-3 hours or the caramel topping will lose its crispness and become soggy.

Lemon Delicious Pudding

Crockpot High 2 ¼-3 hrs	Slow Cooker High 2 ¼-3 hrs

3 eggs, separated

¾ cup sugar

1 tsp grated lemon zest

4 Tbsp lemon juice

1 ½ Tbsp melted butter or margarine

¼ cup plain flour

1 cup milk

Serves 4

This pudding is quite magical. The delicate texture of the softly set sponge topping and the sharp, refreshing lemon flavour of the custard beneath is truly delicious.

1. Pre-heat the cooker for 20 minutes.

2. Butter a 6-cup capacity casserole dish.

3. Beat the egg whites until the peaks fold over when the beater is removed. Set aside.

4. In a separate bowl, beat the egg yolks and sugar until thick and creamy. Add the lemon zest, juice, melted butter, flour and milk.

5. Fold in the egg whites gently but thoroughly.

6. Pour the mixture into the prepared dish, cover tightly with foil and place on trivet in cooker. Pour enough boiling water into the cooker to come half-way up the sides of the casserole dish.

7. Cook following the times and settings above.

8. Let stand for 10 minutes before serving.

9. Serve with cream or ice cream.

Rhubarb and Strawberry Sauce

Crockpot Low 2-3 hrs	Slow Cooker Low 1 ¾-2 ¼ hrs

2 cups fresh or frozen strawberries

450g thinly sliced rhubarb

1 cup sugar

grated zest of one orange

3 Tbsp cornflour

¼ cup orange juice

Serves 4-6

This fruity sauce makes a luscious ice cream topping or can be served by itself topped with a dollop of whipped cream. Don't be tempted to leave out the orange zest as it really enhances the flavour of the strawberries.

1. If the strawberries are fresh, wash and hull. If frozen, thaw. Combine strawberries with the rhubarb in the cooker. If using fresh strawberries, add 2 Tbsp water to the cooker.

2. Add sugar and grated orange zest and stir to combine.

3. Cover with lid and cook following the times and settings above.

4. During the last half hour of cooking, turn the control to high and stir in the cornflour which has been mixed to a paste with the orange juice.

5. Cover with lid and cook for 30 minutes or until mixture has thickened slightly.

Notes

Poached Quinces

Crockpot High approx 3 hrs	Slow Cooker High 2 ¾-3 hrs

1 ½ cups sugar

3 cups boiling water

½ cinnamon stick

5 whole cloves

zest and juice of one lemon

1.75-2.5kg (about 5 large) quinces

Quinces take a long time to cook. Leaving them in a low oven for 4-8 hours is the generally accepted way of poaching them. When cooked in the cooker, the cooking time is approximately 3 hours. As the quinces cook, the colour deepens to a gorgeous reddish apricot. The juice remains beautifully clear whilst taking on the apricot hues.

The fruit will discolour while you are peeling and slicing but as the colour deepens during cooking, the discoloration is not important.

This recipe was developed by Jacqui George, daughter of my dear friend and fellow food writer, Mary Browne.

1. Pre-heat the cooker for 20 minutes.

2. Add the sugar and boiling water and stir until the sugar is dissolved.

3. Add the cinnamon stick, cloves, lemon zest and juice.

4. Peel the quinces and cut each into eighths. Using a sharp knife remove the hard core by cutting downwards onto a board. Discard the cores. Place the quince slices in the syrup in the slow cooker.

5. Cover and cook following the times and settings above.

Apples and Rhubarb with Ginger

Crockpot Low 3-4 hrs	Slow Cooker Low 2 ¾-3 hrs

500g rhubarb, cut into 2-3 cm lengths

500g apples, peeled, cored and sliced

¼ cup finely chopped crystallized ginger

½ cup sugar

½ cup boiling water

Serves 6-8

The apples take on rhubarb's beautiful rose-pink colour and a little of its sweet sharpness.

This is delicious with rich chocolate cakes or as a sauce over ice cream.

1. Pre-heat the cooker for 20 minutes.

2. Place fruit in cooker and stir gently so that the apples and rhubarb are well mixed together.

3. Sprinkle with ginger and sugar. Pour boiling water over.

4. Cover with lid and cook following the times and settings above. The fruit can also be cooked on high for 1-2 hours but tends to lose its shape somewhat.

Notes

Brandy Pot

Crockpot Low 5 ½-6 ½ hrs	Slow Cooker 4 ½-5 ½ hrs

300g dried apricots, halved

300g raisins

150g crystallized ginger, finely chopped

150g dried mango slices, chopped

1 x 425g tin stoneless black cherries in syrup

1 x 425g tin peaches in syrup, chopped

1 x 425g tin pears in syrup, chopped

1 ¼ cups honey

2 ½ cups brandy

¼ cup lemon juice

Makes about 12 cups.

Exotic and rich, this superbly alcoholic fruit makes a divine dessert. Serve over ice cream or pile into tall glasses and drizzle with a little cream.

It is very comforting to have a stash of this in the fridge, as a really glamorous dessert can be produced in relatively quick time with absolutely no effort.

Rum or Brandy Pots usually require several weeks to develop fully, but with the cooker's gentle heat the juices and alcohol mingle and permeate through the fruit very quickly. Refrigerate for 24 hours and your brandy pot will have matured sufficiently for you to imbibe.

1. Place the dried fruit in the cooker.

2. Add the tinned fruit and juice, honey, brandy and lemon juice.

3. Cover with lid and cook following the times and settings above.

4. Allow to cool. Spoon into jars, cover and refrigerate.

The Brandy Pot should keep indefinitely in the fridge.

Notes

Fruity Tipple

Crockpot Low 5-6 hrs	Slow Cooker Low 4 ½-5 hrs

2 large Granny Smith apples, peeled, cored and sliced

200g dried apricots, halved

150g dried peaches chopped

100g glace pineapple, chopped

100g crystallized ginger, chopped

100g raisins

½ cup raw sugar

1 ½ cups sherry

1 ½ cups orange juice

¼ cup lemon juice

¾ cup Earl Grey tea

Serves 9-10.

The taste of this delectable mixture of fresh and dried fruits is heavenly. Serve it over ice cream or with whipped cream or plain unsweetened yoghurt. It keeps well in the fridge.

1. Place the apples on the bottom of the cooker, add the dried fruits and sprinkle with sugar.

2. Combine the sherry, orange juice, lemon juice and tea and pour over the fruit.

3. Cover with lid and cook following the times and settings above.

4. Cool to room temperature and serve.

Notes

Winter Fruit Compote

Crockpot Low 4-5 hrs	Slow Cooker Low 3-4 hrs

4 medium apples, peeled, cored and sliced

½ cup raisins

8 dried figs, sliced

10 prunes, pitted and halved

2 Tbsp lemon juice

¼ tsp ground nutmeg

¼ tsp ground cinnamon

½ cup sugar

1 cup port wine

Serves 6

A rather special dessert which is very easy to prepare and not particularly expensive. The apples absorb the spices, port and some colour from the dried fruit so they darken in colour. Serve with cream, ice cream or Greek yoghurt.

1. Pre-heat the cooker for 20 minutes.

2. Place apples, raisins, figs, and prunes in the cooker.

3. Sprinkle with lemon juice, nutmeg, cinnamon and sugar and pour over the port wine. Stir.

4. Cover the cooker with lid. Cook following the times and settings above.

Notes

Baked Apples

Crockpot Low 6-7 hrs	Slow Cooker Low 5-6 hrs

6 medium apples
(180g each)

6 dates

¾ cup raisins

¾ cup orange or apple juice

3 Tbsp firmly packed brown sugar

¼ tsp ground nutmeg

¼ tsp ground cinnamon

Ice cream or thick yoghurt to serve

___

Serves 6

Choose crisp eating apples as these are less likely to collapse during cooking.

1. Core apples and peel to about one-third down.

2. Push a date into the cored base of each apple. Add raisins and pack firmly into the cored apples.

3. Arrange the apples in the cooker (they may be stacked on each other if necessary) and scatter any remaining raisins around the apples.

4. Pour the juice over and around the apples.

5. Combine the brown sugar, nutmeg and cinnamon and sprinkle over the apples.

6. Cover with lid and cook following the times and settings above or until the apples are tender (depending on size and variety of apples).

7. Serve hot or at room temperature with ice cream or thick yoghurt.

Notes

Baking
Breads and Cakes

There may be times when you prefer not to turn the oven on, or do not have access to one. If on holiday in a caravan or a crib without an oven, it is easy with a slow cooker to produce simple, delicious bread, cakes and fruit loaves.

All baking must be done on high heat and the cooker must be pre-heated for 20 minutes.

A straight-sided casserole dish is an ideal container as is a stainless steel pudding basin. A cake tin can also be used as long as it is watertight. A tin with a removable base is not suitable. Check that the chosen dish will fit comfortably in the slow cooker.

Carrot, Ginger and Lemon Cake

Crockpot High 3-4 hrs	Slow Cooker High 3-4 hrs

60g raisins

¼ cup lemon juice

120g plain flour

1 tsp baking powder

1 tsp baking soda

1 tsp ground cinnamon

100g wholemeal flour

170g raw sugar

250g grated carrot (grated weight)

100g crystallized ginger, chopped

2 eggs (size 6) beaten

3 Tbsp canola oil

Lemon icing

1 ¾ cups icing sugar

2 Tbsp lemon juice (approx)

crystallized ginger, finely chopped to garnish

Serves 10

A beautifully moist, rich-tasting cake with a tangy lemon icing.

Most cakes and pastries are high-energy food, which means that they have a high kilojoule content per unit weight. With only 3 Tbsp of oil and under a cup of sugar this cake has fewer kilojoules than most. Enjoy in moderation.

1. Pre-heat the cooker for 20 minutes.
2. Line the base and sides of a 20cm straight-sided casserole dish with non-stick baking paper.
3. Place the raisins and lemon juice in a small bowl, stir and leave to soak.
4. Sift the flour, baking powder, baking soda and cinnamon into a bowl. Add the wholemeal flour and stir well.
5. Combine the sugar with the grated carrot, stir in the ginger, eggs, oil, raisins and lemon juice.
6. Pour the sugar and carrot mixture into the bowl with the sifted dry ingredients. Mix together well.
7. Spoon the mixture into the casserole dish and cover tightly with foil. Place the dish on a trivet in the cooker. Pour enough boiling water into the cooker to come about half-way up the sides of the dish.
8. Cover with lid and cook following the times and settings above.
9. Lift the dish out of the cooker, remove the foil and allow to cool for about 10 minutes. Slide a knife between the sides of the dish and the cake to loosen it and turn out onto a cake rack. Allow to cool completely.
10. To make the icing, mix the icing sugar with enough of the lemon juice to make an icing of spreadable consistency.
11. Smooth the icing over the cake and sprinkle with the chopped crystallized ginger.

Banana Fruit Loaf

Crockpot High 3-3 ½ hrs	Slow Cooker High 3-3 ½ hrs

150g sugar

130g mixed dried fruit

250ml strong Earl Grey tea, hot

1 Tbsp butter or margarine

1 tsp baking soda

1 egg, size 6, beaten

2 small ripe bananas, mashed (¾ cup)

½ tsp ground nutmeg

½ tsp mixed spice

260g plain flour

2 tsp baking powder

Moist and very low in fat, this is a delicious and healthy alternative to biscuits with your morning coffee.

1. Pre-heat the cooker for 20 minutes.

2. Lightly grease the sides and line the base of a 6-cup capacity casserole dish with non-stick baking paper.

3. Combine the sugar and dried fruit in a bowl and pour over the hot, strong tea, stir in the butter and leave to cool a little.

4. Add the baking soda, egg and the mashed banana and mix well.

5. Add the sifted dry ingredients and stir briefly, just enough to combine.

6. Spoon the mixture into the prepared dish and cover tightly with foil.

7. Place the dish on a trivet in the cooker.

8. Pour enough boiling water into the cooker to come half-way up the sides of the dish.

9. Cover with lid and cook following the times and settings above.

10. Lift the dish out of the cooker. Remove the foil and allow to cool for about 10 minutes. Loosen edges with knife and invert the loaf onto a cake cooler and allow to cool completely.

Pumpernickel Bread

Crockpot High 4 ½-5 hrs	Slow Cooker High 4 ½-5 hrs

3 cups rye flour

1 cup kibbled rye

1 cup kibbled wheat

½ tsp salt

2 Tbsp treacle

2 Tbsp cooking oil

¼ cup bran

3 cups boiling water

wholemeal flour for shaping (¾-1 cup)

The perfect bread to accompany cheese, salami and beer. As it has no leavening, it is a heavy dark bread which slices beautifully. This recipe is from the New Zealand Bread Book by Mary Browne, Helen Leach and Nancy Titchborne. I have changed the method of cooking to suit the slow cooker.

1. Mix all the ingredients together to form a thick drop batter. Cover the bowl and leave overnight.

2. Next morning pre-heat the cooker for 20 minutes.

3. Line the base of a casserole dish or cake tin (7-cup capacity) which will fit into the cooker, with non-stick baking paper.

4. Turn the dough out onto a floured board and add sufficient wholemeal flour to be able to handle the dough. Shape into a loaf.

5. Place the loaf into the prepared dish or tin and cover the top with a round of non-stick baking paper. This will prevent the bread from sticking to the foil.

6. Cover the container tightly with foil. Place the container on a trivet in the cooker.

7. Cover with the lid and cook following the times and settings above. Remove foil and baking paper for the last 5 minutes of baking.

8. Lift the container from the cooker, remove the foil and blot the top of the loaf with a paper towel. The top may look a little damp but it will dry out.

9. Cool before wrapping in greaseproof paper and then in foil. Store unused portions in the fridge.

Boston Brown Bread

Crockpot High 4-5 hrs	Slow Cooker High 4-5 hrs

1 cup wholemeal flour

1 cup rye flour

1 cup fine cornmeal

2 tsp baking soda

½ tsp salt

¼ cup treacle

¼ cup golden syrup

¼ cup brown sugar, firmly packed

2 Tbsp butter

1 ½ cups milk

1 Tbsp white vinegar

1 cup raisins

This is an adaptation of a traditional American bread which is usually eaten with baked beans. Rich and dark, it has a nutty texture. It is excellent spread with butter for afternoon tea or school lunches. The leftovers make delicious toast.

1. Pre-heat the cooker for 20 minutes.
2. Grease an 8-cup capacity stainless steel basin (the batter should not fill more than two-thirds of the basin).
3. Combine the wholemeal flour, rye flour, cornmeal, baking soda and salt in a large bowl.
4. Melt the treacle, syrup, sugar and butter until just runny. Remove from the heat and add milk and vinegar.
5. Make a well in the centre of the dry ingredients and pour in the treacle milk mixture. Add the raisins.
6. Stir until all ingredients are combined.
7. Pour into the greased basin and cover tightly with foil. Place basin on trivet in cooker.
8. Pour enough boiling water around the basin to come half-way up the side.
9. Cover cooker with lid and cook following the times and settings above.
10. Lift the basin from the cooker and remove foil.
11. Allow to cool for about 10 minutes. Turn bread out onto a wire rack.

Corn Bread

Crockpot High 2 ½-2 ¾ hrs	Slow Cooker High 2 ½-2 ¾ hrs

1 cup plain flour

1 cup coarse cornmeal

1 tsp baking powder

½ tsp baking soda

⅛ tsp cayenne pepper

½ tsp salt

½ cup grated tasty cheese

2 eggs, beaten

¾ cup cream style corn

½ cup plain unsweetened yoghurt

2 Tbsp oil

2 Tbsp milk

1 Tbsp brown sugar

This American style corn bread is a perfect accompaniment to soups, stews and salads. Coarse cornmeal gives it an interesting gritty texture and cream style corn adds extra flavour and moistness.

1. Pre-heat cooker for 20 minutes.

2. Lightly oil the sides and line the base of a 6-cup capacity casserole dish with non-stick baking paper.

3. In a bowl place the flour, cornmeal, baking powder, baking soda, cayenne pepper and salt and mix well. Add the cheese and stir. Set aside.

4. In a small bowl combine the eggs, cream style corn, yoghurt, oil, milk and brown sugar and mix well.

5. Tip the egg mixture into the dry ingredients and stir until just moistened. Too much stirring develops the gluten in the flour and makes for tough bread.

6. Pour this mixture into the prepared dish. Cover tightly with foil and place the dish on a trivet in the cooker. Pour enough boiling water around it to come half-way up the dish.

7. Cover with lid and cook following the times and settings above.

8. Lift out of the cooker and remove foil. Allow to cool for about 10 minutes. Loosen edges with a knife. Invert onto a cake rack and allow to cool completely.

9. Serve buttered.

Interesting Extras

Lemon Curd

Crockpot Low 3-4 hrs	Slow Cooker Low 3-4 hrs

60g butter

350g sugar

2 cups lemon juice

4 large eggs, beaten

Velvety and tart, this lovely lemon curd is a great preserve to have in the fridge. Try it on toasted bagels, atop a pavlova and of course as a filling for lemon tarts.

1. Pre-heat the cooker for 20 minutes.

2. While cooker is heating, melt the butter either in a saucepan (not aluminium) or in a microwave oven.

3. Stir in the sugar and lemon juice and heat just enough for the sugar to dissolve. Leave to cool for about 10 minutes.

4. Sieve the eggs through a plastic or stainless steel sieve into the sugar and lemon juice mixture.

5. Pour into a 5-6 cup casserole dish which will fit into the cooker (stainless steel tends to get too hot so I prefer to use Pyrex or oven-proof china).

6. Cover the dish tightly with foil, place on a trivet in the cooker and pour enough boiling water into the cooker to come half-way up the sides of the casserole dish.

7. Cover with lid and cook for 3-4 hours until the liquid thickens. If convenient stir once or twice during the cooking time.

8. Pour the lemon curd into clean jars, cover and store in the fridge and use within 4 weeks.

9. Makes approximately 4 x 250 ml jars.

Wholegrain Oat Porridge

Crockpot Low 8-10 hrs	Slow Cooker Low 8-10 hrs

½ cup wholegrain oats
pinch salt
1 cup milk
1 cup water

Serves 2

The cooker cooks porridge to perfection – smooth and deliciously creamy. The porridge thickens with the long, slow cooking, more than it would if cooked conventionally. It's worth making the effort before you go to bed to organize this – a couple of minutes is all it takes.

There is increasing evidence that a diet rich in whole grains may give some protection against heart disease and help lower blood cholesterol levels. Wholegrain oat porridge, cooked overnight, is a quick, easy and nutritious start to the day.

The proportion of milk to water can be altered to suit your taste.

For example, use all milk or all water if you prefer as long as the liquid totals 2 cups.

1. Place wholegrain oats in a small casserole dish (4-5 cup capacity) and add the salt, milk and water.

2. Cover with foil or a plate.

3. Place on a trivet in the cooker and pour enough cold water into the cooker to come half-way up the casserole dish.

4. Cook following the times and directions above.

5. Add your favourite topping, milk, honey or brown sugar.

Mulled Wine

Crockpot High for 1 hr reduce to low for 3-4 hrs	Slow Cooker High for 1 hr reduce to low for 3-4 hrs

2 medium oranges

6 cloves

2 cups cranberry juice, warmed

4 cups red wine

½ cup brandy

½ cup caster sugar

1 cinnamon stick

5 cardamom pods, lightly crushed

Makes 8-10 glasses.

Mulled wine is a heady drink for a chilly winter's night.

This is a beautiful, rich magenta colour and wonderfully aromatic.

1. Pre-heat the cooker.

2. Rinse or scrub the oranges and stud one with whole cloves.

3. Place the studded orange in the cooker and add the warmed cranberry juice, red wine, brandy, and sugar. Stir.

4. Break the cinnamon stick in half and add to the cooker with the cardamom pods.

5. Cover with lid and cook following the times and settings above.

6. To serve, remove the clove-studded orange and the pieces of cinnamon stick.

7. Slice the remaining orange and float the slices on top of wine. Ladle into warm stemmed glasses.

Notes

Hot Spiced Cider

Crockpot High for 1 hr then reduce to low for 3-4 hrs	Slow Cooker High for 1 hr then reduce to low for 3-4 hrs

1 orange

1 lemon

8 whole cloves

1 cup orange juice, warmed

1 cup pineapple juice, warmed

1 x 1.5 litre bottle apple cider

¼ cup caster sugar

2 cinnamon sticks

Makes 10-12 glasses

The flavour of the pineapple and orange is apparent but not dominant in this spicy mulled cider.

1. Pre-heat the cooker for 20 minutes.

2. Rinse or scrub the orange and the lemon. Set lemon aside.

3. Cut the orange into quarters and stud each segment with two cloves.

4. Place the orange segments, orange juice, pineapple juice, apple cider and sugar in the cooker and stir.

5. Break the cinnamon sticks in half and add to the cooker.

6. Cover with lid and cook following the times and settings above.

7. Remove the clove-studded orange segments and the pieces of cinnamon stick.

8. Slice the lemon and float the slices on top of the cider and ladle into warm stemmed glasses.

Notes

Index